Images of a People

IMAGES OF A PEOPLE
Tlingit Myths and Legends

Mary Helen Pelton
and
Jacqueline DiGennaro

Illustrated by
Jennifer Brady-Morales
(*Ts'anak*)

1992
Libraries Unlimited, Inc.
Englewood, Colorado

LIBRARIES UNLIMITED, INC.
P.O. Box 6633
Englewood, CO 80155-6633

Interior book design and type selection by Judy Gay Matthews.

Library of Congress Cataloging-in-Publication Data

Pelton, Mary Helen White.
   Images of a people : Tlingit myths and legends / Mary Helen Pelton
and Jacqueline DiGennaro ; illustrated by Jennifer Brady-Morales
(Ts'anak)
   xvii, 170 p. 19x26 cm.
   Includes bibliographical references (p. 161) and index.
   ISBN 0-87287-918-6
   1. Tlingit Indians--Social life and customs. 2. Tlingit Indians-
-Legends. I. DiGennaro, Jacqueline. II. Title.
E99.T6P45 1992
398.2'089972--dc20   92-20564
                                                              CIP

We dedicate this book to our parents:

Helen Peek Hamilton
and the late
James B. Hamilton, Sr.,

who gave us the love of story.

Contents

Part 2
THE STORIES

Preface

*Before there was a North or South
when Time was not
Klingaton-kla, the Earth Mother
was blind and all the world was dark.*

—J. Frederic Thorne
(*In the Time That Was;
Being Legends of the Alaska Klingits*)

As the grandmother wove the banded basket with swift and practiced hands, the dark-haired child leaned closer. The story was about to begin....

Then ashes was I, for not yet was I born. This was a time before time; a time when Raven was white and all the world was clothed in darkness....

The story unfolded and the child and the grandmother experienced once again the wondrous connection of storyteller and listener—the enduring oral tradition of many cultures.

The Tlingit* are native people of southeastern Alaska (see map on page 35). Like many other cultures, they had no written language for many years. Their history, beliefs, traditions, and values were passed from one generation to the next through their strong oral tradition. Studying their stories teaches us about the people, and a knowledge of the people helps us understand their stories. This book provides both perspectives. Like mirrors facing each other, these two reflected images take us deeper and deeper into a sense of the people called Tlingit.

---

*Tlingit is pronounced phonetically except for the initial character. The sound of the initial character is made by putting your tongue behind your teeth and forcing air out of either side of the tongue to produce a gutteral sound which most closely resembles a gutteral **K** in English.

Some Tlingit are moving away from spelling their tribal name in the traditional way with a **T**, favoring *Lingit.* However, in this book, we have retained the traditional spelling.

THE BOOK

The Tlingit culture has strong kinship bonds, dramatic art forms, and a strong spiritualism. The first part of the book explores Tlingit history and land; kinship and social structure; ceremonies; values; spiritualism, religion and cosmology; the Kushtaka (terrifying supernatural creatures who stalked the earth looking for human captives); shamanism; witchcraft; and art forms such as the giant totems, spruce root basketry, and bentwood boxes. Cultural themes, reflected in the stories, are looked at first in part 1.

Illustrated by traditional Tlingit artist, Jennifer Brady-Morales (*Ts'anak* in Tlingit), the second part of the book has twenty-two myths and legends. Myths, and their power, are important. Joseph Campbell says:

> Throughout the inhabited world, in all times and under every circumstance, the myths of man have flourished; and they have been the living inspiration of whatever else may have appeared out of the activities of the human body and mind. It would not be too much to say that myth is the secret opening into human manifestation. Religions, philosophies, arts, and social forms of primitive and historic man, prime discoveries in science and technology, the very dreams that blister sleep, boil up from the basic, magic ring of myth (1968, 3).

To the Tlingit, as to all people of the world, stories convey the traditions, values, fears, spiritual beliefs, and world view of a culture to adults and children alike. Bill Moyers, interviewing Campbell in *The Power of Myth*, says, "What human beings have in common is revealed in myths. Myths are our search through the ages for truth, for meaning, for significance. We all need to tell our story and to understand our story" (1988, 5). The stories tell us about the people.

The stories we have included may illustrate both Tlingit and mythological themes containing universal truths that reach far beyond the Tlingit culture. These are not only Tlingit myths and legends but stories of all humankind.

In researching the first part, we used materials spanning two centuries. The early missionaries, anthropologists, and ethnographers in Alaska were European or American and viewed the Tlingit culture through their own cultural perspectives. Their writings and research are balanced by the research of Nora Marks Dauenhauer and Richard Dauenhauer, giving the Tlingit perspective. Nora Marks Dauenhauer, a Tlingit, completed the transcription, translation, and annotation of their field research and provided the cultural background for their works. Her husband, Richard Dauenhauer, a former poet laureate of Alaska with a doctorate in comparative literature, provided expertise in grammar and lent a particular style to their writings.

In doing our research we sometimes found conflicting opinion among the sources we explored. In these instances we use the source that seems the most authoritative. If neither of two conflicting viewpoints seem more authoritative, both viewpoints are presented. Cross checking the information with the most knowledgeable of the Tlingit elders was almost impossible. The elders were unwilling to talk. We tried to verify information from the Tlingit perspective with the Sitka Native Educational Program, a Tlingit organization, but were told that the information could not be made available. The Dauenhauers' book explains such resistance: "Because books are alien to Tlingit education and because many negative and inaccurate things have been written about the Tlingit culture, there was, and still is, great suspicion of and even hostility toward books and literacy among members of the older generation of Tlingits" (1990, xi).

Being unable to read or write Tlingit, we used documents either written in or translated into English. The Tlingit language is very rich. For example, in English we have only one word for *rain*; however, the Tlingit language has many words depending on the nature of the rain. English cannot capture all the complexity and the subtle nuances of Tlingit language, but readers will enjoy much of the cultural richness nonetheless.

We have treated the culture with as much respect as we are able and would like to have offered more original Tlingit sources, but all information available is presented as carefully and conscientiously as possible.

In part 2, all the stories except "The Girl Who Married a Bear" were based on John Swanton's work for the Smithsonian Institution entitled *Tlingit Myths and Texts* (1909). Swanton appears to be one of the most complete and least culturally biased of the early writers. Swanton was an ethnologist who recorded the myths at Sitka and Wrangell, Alaska, from January through April of 1904. Swanton's sources are indicated at the end of each story. The story "The Girl Who Married a Bear" is found in many sources including De Laguna (1972) and McClellan (1970). Similar stories were collected by others who came later.

We have tried to retain the original meaning and emphasis of the stories, but they have been shaped to make them more "round." Many of the stories were told originally by the Tlingit as long tales with new "chapters" added each evening; therefore, sometimes narratives, in written form, seem to drift off without a satisfactory conclusion. We wanted the stories to stand alone, so each story was brought to a conclusion consistent with the intent of the tale.

COMPARATIVE THEMES

Although these are Tlingit tales, many of the threads that run through them are found in the folk literature of many cultures. We are all truly a part of the family of humankind linked together by an ancient history. The universal themes are outlined briefly so students of folk literature can watch for them:

- The main character must survive four tests to win the maiden: "Little Felon."

- Time passes while the main character is on his quest, a day in the land beyond is a year on earth: "The Wolf Chief's Son."

- A hero is born of a virgin: "Raven Steals the Light" and "I Am Strength."

- A spirit helper gives the hero three objects to help him escape the evil powers: "The Boy Who Shot the Star."

- Life is a circle; when one thing dies another replaces it: "The Image That Came to Life."

- The hero must make the journey to the land beyond and return: "Return from the Spirit Land."

- The lazy will come to ill: "The Man Who Was Abandoned."

- The Brer Rabbit theme—"Don't throw me into the briar patch, anything but the briar patch": "The Sky Country."

For the convenience of the reader the authors have grouped the stories according to five major themes:

- The Creation and Why Things Came to Be
- The World of the Spirits
- The Animal Spirit Helper
- Stories That Teach the Values of the Culture
- Kushtaka and Witches

Several of the stories could have been placed in more than one group; therefore, the authors assigned the story by its major theme.

The Creation and Why Things Came to Be. While in the Tlingit world view there was no great god, there was a mythical character, Raven, who was born of a virgin. This powerful benefactor brought light to a world immersed in darkness. Many stories of Raven the benefactor and Raven the trickster exist. However, we include only one of Raven's many adventures in "Raven Steals the Light." The other three stories in this section have a "how-and-why" theme. All cultures have tales that explain how things came to be, for example, Kipling's "How the Elephant Got His Trunk"; the African "How All the Stories Came to Be"; the Norwegian "Why the Sea Is Salty"; the Hmong "Why the Hmong Live on Mountains"; and the Iroquois "Why the Owl Has Big Eyes." In the Tlingit tale "The Origin of the Killer Whale," the reader not only learns where killer whales came from but discovers the reason for the great animosity between the shark and the killer whale. The origin of the little white tuft on the head of the puffin is revealed in "The Story of the Puffin." "Beaver and Porcupine" explains why the beaver and porcupine are no longer friends.

The World of the Spirits. The spiritual journey, the mythological journey to the land of the dead and back again, is widely discussed in comparative literature, mythology, and religion. This archetypical journey is described by Joseph Campbell.

> The standard of the mythological adventure of the hero is a magnification of the formula representing the rites of passage: separation-initiation-return. A hero ventures forth from the world of common day into the region of supernatural wonder: fabulous forces are encountered there and a decisive victory is won: the hero comes back from this mysterious adventure with the power to bestow boons on his fellow man (1968, 35).

The Tlingit myth "Return from the Spirit Land" describes such a journey. A man travels to the land of the dead to bring back his beloved wife.

The tales of many cultures feature *mythological* characters moving between the land of the living and the land of the dead. The dead come back to stay among the living in two stories, "The Woman Who Married the Dead Man" and "The Image That Came to Life." The blurring between the earth and the world above is described in "The Sky Country." If a man is powerful enough to defeat a great spirit creature, then he is powerful enough to take that spirit as part of himself. This is the theme of "The Origin of Gonaqadē't, Monster of the Sea."

The Animal Spirit Helper. According to Tlingit myths, animals and spirits looked and lived like human beings. They could understand what people said and might at times take human form. They would punish those who mistreated them and reward those who did not. In "The Wolf Chief's Son," "The Story of the Eagle Crest of the Nexa'di," "The Man Who Was Abandoned," and "Little Felon," animal helpers appear to assist humans in various ways.

Stories That Teach the Values of the Culture. Even when a Tlingit is alone, an individual must not speak ill of any living thing. The spirits are everywhere and punishment for an unkind remark will be swift. In "The Girl Who Married a Bear" and "The Boy Who Shot the Star," the main characters do not adhere to this cultural imperative and are punished.

Boys must go through rigorous training to be strong and brave. In "I Am Strength," the boy endures the hardship of freezing water to gain the strength that will save his people.

Many cultures have cautionary tales which warn, "Be good to the rich and poor alike for one day you may be poor." "The Orphan" is such a cautionary tale.

The Tlingits believe, "Take only what you need. Return your gifts to mother earth and you will be twice rewarded." The sisters in "The Mountain Dweller" are gluttonous and are banished from their families. The man in "The Salmon Chief" treats the remains of the salmon with respect and he is rewarded.

The spiritual bond between humans and animals is demonstrated in "The Man Who Entertained the Bears." The story also suggests that we must be willing to share with friends and foes alike.

Kushtaka and Witches. The Tlingits' fear of the Kushtaka, also referred to as the Land Otter People, and of witches is real and borders on terror. Two stories about these fearful creatures are included, "Kushtaka's Captive" and "The Faithless Wife."

This book will appeal to a broad range of readers: folklorists, storytellers, teachers, children, librarians, people interested in other cultures and comparative literature, visitors to the land of the Tlingit, residents of the northwestern United States, artists, and people who just plain enjoy a good story.

Acknowledgments

We would like to express grateful appreciation to the following people who helped with our project:

Peter Corey, curator of collections at Sheldon Jackson Museum, Sitka, Alaska, for his advice and expertise concerning the customs and artwork of the Tlingit people and for his reading of the story section. His insight and support were invaluable to the writing of the book.

Dan Evans, who generously contributed several beautiful color photographs to the project.

Jim DiGennaro, for creating "computer literate" writers out of "one-finger" typists, for his photography work, and for the map of southeast Alaska (see page 35).

Nancy Ricketts, archival librarian at Sheldon Jackson College's Stratton Library, who helped enormously with the research on the book.

Cicely Muldoon, curator at Sitka National Historical Park, for patiently poring over historical photographs with us.

Teri Rofkar, for sharing her knowledge of spruce root basketry.

Ray Pelton, for his insightful critique, which helped us clarify and strengthen the manuscript.

The People, the Land, and History

The word *Tlingit* means "the people." These are the "people" of southeastern Alaska, the people of the totem. The culture of the Tlingit is rich, shaped by the land, the climate, their history, their beliefs, their social structure, and their stories. The stories cannot and do not stand apart from the rich texture of their lives. Rather, the stories reflect the culture, and the culture is reflected in the stories. To fully appreciate the stories, it is important to first know the people.

A 27-foot tall totem pole carved in 1976 depicts 200 years of the cultural history of the Pacific Northwest Coast Indians. The totem (see page 37), located in Sitka National Historical Park, Sitka, Alaska, tells this story:

> In the time before the coming of the white man, the Northwest Coast Indians lived in close harmony with nature, sharing a rich material culture and ceremonial life. The base figure of the totem holds a halibut hook and the ceremonial rattle. The halibut hook is designed to insure that small fish cannot take the hook. Thus, only those fish of appropriate size can be caught and the little ones are left to keep nature in balance. The ceremonial rattle shows the people's respect for the spirits that are in all things.
>
> On the next section is carved the Raven and the Eagle, the two major symbols of the Tlingit people. They hold a copper shield used in inter-tribal commerce and three salmon symbolizing abundant food resources.
>
> On top of the Raven and Eagle stands a figure symbolizing the arrival of the white man, bringing with him firearms, documents, and Christianity. The white man's guns and his god defeated the Tlingit. In his right hand he holds a rolled document, signifying a long line of treaties.

The top figure shows the Northwest Coast Indian of today. He weighs his values—the old way against the new, the effect of technology and industry on the people and on the environment. The figure holds two long poles. The staff on the left is richly carved reflecting the texture of the cultural past. The staff on the right represents the future, thus it is yet to be carved (Alaska Natural History Association 1980).

EARLY IMMIGRANTS

Before people measured time, small groups of Neolithic hunters crossed from the Asian continent to the North American continent over a land bridge in western Alaska. Later the land bridge would disappear, and the subsequent water passage would be named the Bering Strait. Wave after wave of immigrants came. As the last great Ice Age drew to a close and the glaciers receded, the ancestors of the Tlingit people reached what we call the Queen Charlotte Islands in approximately 6000 B.C.

As time went on, the Tlingits established their territory. Most of the early reports suggest that the Tlingits occupied the Alaskan panhandle from 54 to 60 degrees latitude, which begins north of the Queen Charlotte Islands and ends just north of Yakutat Bay (see map on page 35). This magnificent rugged coast of southeastern Alaska became the home of the Tlingit people. Now, as in those earlier times, the mountains seem to rise from the sea. The summits are clothed in everlasting snows, and the mountain slopes are covered in dense spruce, fir, hemlock, pine, and cedar forests. Retreating glaciers left sculpted landscapes, creating inlets and fiords, which intrude into the seemingly impenetrable range. (See color photographs on pages 43 and 44.)

A fringe of innumerable islands protects the mainland from the open seas. These mountainous and heavily forested buffers include such large islands as Vancouver, Queen Charlotte, Prince of Wales, Baranof, and Chichagof, and waterways such as Portland Canal, Lynn Canal, and Taku Inlet.

The weather of the Tlingits' coastal homeland was surprisingly mild for a land so far north. (The National Park Service, in its brochure on Sitka National Historical Park, today describes the weather as "always autumn.") The comfortable conditions were due in part to the moderating influence of the Japanese current. Present-day Sitka, for example, has an average summer temperature of 60 degrees F and a winter temperature of 42 degrees F. Farther inland, the weather became more extreme with summer temperatures averaging about 70 degrees F and 80 degrees F or more in the valleys leading into the interior. Winter temperatures then, and today, were likewise variable, with colder temperatures reported inland.

The mountains, the fiords, and the meandering beauty of the inland passageway were not the only startling features of the southeastern Alaskan landscape. Tremendous stands of Sitka spruce and western hemlock thrived in the abundant rainfall, averaging over 100 inches a year. These unbroken stands towered to heights of 200 feet or more. When these overmature giants fell, they created gaps in the forest canopy. As the understory responded to increased sunlight, wildlife populations of deer and bear flourished in the new ecologically diverse environment.

The rugged land did not support agriculture, and the dense forests and high mountains made the interior almost impenetrable. Therefore, the people settled along the coastline in sheltered coves and inlets where they could farm the sea. The land and the sea were so abundant that they had to struggle minimally for existence. Southeastern Alaskan waters are still said to be among the richest fishing grounds in the world. Shellfish, halibut, bottom fish, sea lions, and seals can be taken year-round. During the late summer and fall, salmon ascend the streams to spawn. Smoked salmon continues to provide a major food staple. In the spring the people harvest herring, herring eggs, sea bird eggs, sprouts from plants, and eulachon (candle fish), a major source of oil. Bear, deer, and mountain goat may still provide food and in the past were a source of clothing. In July and August berries of many varieties abound.

The abundance of game and fish enabled the people to gather food for an entire year in a few months and allowed them the leisure to develop complex and unique art forms. The art of the Tlingit is discussed in more detail later in this section.

The people lived in massive houses of logs and planking in settlements on sheltered coves and on the banks of rivers. As many as thirty people in a family group lived together in these dwellings. When the salmon were running, temporary fishing camps were set up along various rivers and streams.

The Tlingits had highly developed seamanship skills. In their own waters the Tlingits' skills outshone those of white explorers. They reportedly traveled in their dugout canoes as far away as Puget Sound, a 1,000-mile journey. The Tlingits traded with neighboring tribes: the Tsimshians to the south, the inland Athapascans, and the nearby Haidas.

EUROPEANS ARRIVE

The first Europeans came to the area in search of the Northwest Passage, which supposedly connected the Atlantic and the Pacific Oceans. The first definite accounts of the Tlingits of the Northwest Coast appeared in 1741.

An expedition led by Vitus Bering was organized to explore the North American continent in what Polly Miller and Leon Miller call a "massive and brilliant effort towards scientific discovery" (1967, 4). Bering commanded two ships, the *St. Paul* and the *St. Peter*, during this phase of the exploration. On July 17, 1741, the captain of the *St. Paul*, Alexei Chirikov, sent a group of men to explore the shore at the site of what is modern-day Sitka. When the group did not return, a rescue party was sent. They too disappeared. Later, two canoes manned with natives approached the Russian ship, but when they saw the Russians on the forward deck, they rowed back to land and were not seen again. The diaries about this exploration provide the first written account of the Tlingit.

During the last quarter of the eighteenth century, English, American, French, and Russian fur traders, explorers, and whalers visited and traded with the Tlingit. Pelts of sea otter, beaver, fox, and black bear brought an excellent price at European markets. These visitors had little impact on the Tlingit culture except to give the native people a taste for unfamiliar goods such as tobacco, sugar, and firearms. But, toward the end of the century, friction developed. A Russian trading firm, called the Russian-American Company, was chartered. All other trading firms in the area were ordered to merge with the Russian-American Company or go out of business.

Alexander Baranov was given a substantial share of the stock in the new trading company and was appointed its governor. In 1795 he traveled to Yakutat Bay to establish a Russian colony. Planting the flag and crest of the Russian Empire, he claimed the coastline for the Empress Catherine II. The Tlingits barely tolerated these uninvited guests. Although the trade relationship between the Russian-American Company and the people seemed mutually beneficial, the uneasy peace foundered. In 1802, warriors of the Tlingit Kiksadi clan attacked Redoubt

St. Michael, a Russian outpost, killing nearly all the Aleuts and Russians at the settlement. Late in September of 1804, the Russians counterattacked and recaptured the fort. Although the next quarter century was marked by numerous skirmishes, the 1804 Battle of Sitka, as it was called, was the last major Tlingit resistance. Tlingit culture had become increasingly affected by these unwanted foreigners.

The way of life of the Tlingit was challenged not only by guns, but by the "word" of religious missionaries. In 1824 Father Ivan Veniaminov was sent to the Aleutian Islands. He learned the Aleut language and gained the trust of the people. Aurel Krause, writing in 1885, said, "More than anyone else Veniaminov was concerned with gaining an understanding of the character, customs and habits of the Tlingit" ([1885] 1956, 43). He established a school and began the work of "converting the natives." Despite an impressive stature (he was six feet three inches tall) and a friendly and understanding manner, he won few converts to Christianity until the smallpox epidemic of 1836. The epidemic substantially changed how the Tlingit viewed their world. The epidemic is discussed later in this section.

In 1840 another early missionary, Anatolei Kamenskii, wrote about the Tlingit. In the notes of Sergei Kan, a Kamenskii translator, she says, "Like most Russian missionaries, Kamenskii admired the Tlingits' industriousness, their hunting, fishing and commercial skills, their excellent craftsmanship, their physical stamina, and their oratorical skills. He also admired the position of women in the Tlingit family and their treatment of children (Kamenskii 1985, 9). Veniaminov also spoke favorably of the Tlingit, calling them "the most gifted of the coastal people" (Krause 1956, 104).

The press of hunters and traders changed the environment dramatically in less than one lifetime. By 1850 overhunting had diminished the number of fur seals and sea otters in the north Pacific. Because of the declining economic value of the area and a number of difficulties at home, the distant colony had less and less interest to the Czar. In 1867 he sold Russia's American holdings to the United States for $7.2 million. The natives received no mention in the transaction.

Soon after the purchase, new white settlers came. They established schools and churches. Tlingit children were required to attend schools where only English was taught. In spite of this requirement, the Tlingits held on to their culture and their language. They did not isolate themselves but began to learn how to turn "white man's law" to their own advantage. The Dauenhauers write:

> But in the 1910's and 1920's, Tlingit language and cultural identity were still strong, despite language policies of the government schools. The Native people of Southeast Alaska were involved with other socio-political issues; they campaigned for citizenship, for integrated schools, and for laws prohibiting discrimination in public places; they fought against the use of fish traps. These were challenges to physical and economic survival greater than anything experienced during the Russian period. Many people are unaware that Native Americans were not granted United States citizenship until 1924, and that schools and public facilities, such as restaurants and theaters in Alaska, were segregated until 1945 (1990, 30).

Today, many Tlingits live in the traditional way following the customs and traditions of their ancestors; others do not. Among the Tlingits, as among all the people of Alaska, there are fishers, doctors, teachers, artists, accountants, lawyers, writers, and craftspersons. For the purpose of this book, we look at the traditional way, for it is through this rich tradition that the stories are understood, and it is through the stories that one understands the tradition.

The People and the Social Structure

efore the smallpox epidemic in 1836, Veniaminov estimated that there were about 10,000 people, including the Kaigani of Haida origin, on Prince Wales Island. Approximately one-half of the people died in the smallpox epidemic. According to the 1880 census, the number, excluding the Kaigani, was 6,763 (Krause 1956, 63). In the 1930s the number of Tlingits began to increase again. Today, Judy George of the Central Council of Tlingit and Haida Tribes of Alaska reports that there are 18,872 Tlingits; 4,759 of those live in Anchorage, Seattle, and California (1992).

MOIETIES

The history and mythology of the people can only be fully understood through an examination of their kinship system. Tlingit society is divided into two reciprocating divisions called moieties. The two moieties are named Raven and Eagle. Raven is sometimes known as Crow, and Eagle is sometimes known as Wolf. The moieties have no political organization or power but exist to regulate marriage and to exchange certain death rituals (Dauenhauer and Dauenhauer 1990, 6). Tlingit culture is matrilineal (organized through the mother's line). A Tlingit is born into the mother's moiety, clan, and house group. This does not mean that the society is matriarchal; quite the contrary, the Tlingit culture exhibits a decidedly masculine bias.

Traditionally, a Raven must marry an Eagle. To marry within one's own moiety, for an Eagle to marry an Eagle, or a Raven a Raven, was viewed as incest. Today, marriage within the moiety, as well as marriage to non-Tlingits, is accepted.

CLANS

Each moiety is made of many clans or sibs. Some of these are

Eagle Moiety	Raven Moiety
Wolf	Sea Lion
Brown Bear	Frog
Killer Whale	Beaver
Brown Bear	Goose
Shark	Coho (Silver Salmon)
"Alk"	Sockeye (Red Salmon)
	Dog Salmon

Loyalty to the clan was paramount. Clanship dictated choice of mates, social behavior, and hundreds of other things. Political organization rested at the clan level. Each clan had its own heraldic crests, personal names, and other property. De Laguna said,

> To the native, the nations or sibs of the Tlingit are not only deeply rooted in the mythical past, they are embodiments today of the very origins of the world and of humanity reflecting the natural order and linking of men to it by totemic bonds. The sibs constitute the eternal and unchanging order of the Tlingit people, fixed because no individual can exchange or lose his sib identity and because a sib can never, in theory, be changed except through the total annililation of all its members (1972, 211).

One of the stories that follows is about an orphan. In the Tlingit culture, to be an orphan is a terrible and unusual thing for it means that a person's entire clan has been destroyed.

Clan members recognize their common kinship even though they may be scattered throughout different villages. The traditions of most clans usually refer to the site of their ancestral house. The Tlingits equate the word *tribe* with the words *clan* or *sib*. For English-speaking people this may be confusing because tribe usually refers to those people occupying a certain territory. This has been the source of endless confusion in U.S. government legal documents.

Each clan has a traditional leader, although there is no one leader for the Raven or the Eagle moiety. The Dauenhauers explain: "The Tlingit terms for leaders include *hít sʼaatí* (house master or house leader) *naa shuháni* (one who stands at the head of the clan) and *ḵáa sháadei háni* (leader; one who stands at the head of men). The word *chief* is an American and Russian innovation" (1990, 7-8). This leader has nominal decision-making authority. Krause said, "Only in cooperative undertakings and in council is he a leader, in everything else every family head is entirely free to do anything which is not counter to custom and which does not infringe on the rights of others" (1956, 77). The status of the chief is related to his generosity. The meaning and importance of status will be discussed later in this section. In the stories that follow, the word *chief* is used; however, the reader is reminded that the writers are referring to a chief as Tlingit culture defines it.

Clans traditionally included many house groups. The term *house group* is perhaps a difficult concept because it applies to both kinship and residence. The Dauenhauers say, "It is best to understand house groups as a kinship term, realizing that not all members of a house group physically reside in the ancestral house, that nonresidents of a clan house are members of that house and most of the original houses are no longer standing" (1990, 8). The Dauenhauers continue to explain that the genealogical awareness of the house group has been lost in recent times due to changes in physical housing influenced by missionaries and other social changes in the twentieth century. The effect has been a rise in single-family dwellings and the demise of traditional community houses.

Ano-tlush, "chief" or "headman" of the Taku clan. (Photograph courtesy of the Case and Draper Collection, Alaska Historical Library, Juneau, Alaska.)

FAMILY

The most basic of the social structures is, of course, the family. The family consists of a husband, his wife or wives, and their children. This was, in traditional Tlingit culture, the least significant group politically, since a man and his children were always from different moieties. The basic economic activity of the people was carried out within the family group. Families lived in massive, carefully crafted, permanent plank dwellings. As many as thirty members of the extended family and their slaves lived within these houses.

Children were well loved and cared for in the Tlingit household. As young children, boys and girls played as all children but helped their parents as much as their maturity allowed. This pattern changed as the children grew older because more time went to their education. Children were born into their mother's moiety, clan, and house group. Since tradition dictated that a husband and wife must come from different moieties, a man's children were not his own, but rather, the children of his wife's moiety and clan.

The lineage of the children had implications for the education of children, particularly of sons. Tlingits placed great importance on the proper education of children in the history, manners, and customs of the clan. The father was not qualified to carry out this important function since he was not from his child's moiety or clan. Therefore, at about age six or seven, boys went to stay permanently with one of their mother's brothers, and there they learned the lore, the customs, and the history of their moiety and clan. In addition, young men were taught the use of medicinal plants, animal lore, fishing and seamanship skills, and the use of weapons. The training of young men was physically rigorous to help the boys gain strength. Self-discipline was taught and expected. In the story "I Am Strength," the old man trains the boy as an uncle might. He requires the boy to sit for long periods of time in cold water to build up strength. At the uncle's death, the nephew inherits the uncle's property, possessions, and his wife. Thus, in the story "The Orphan," the main character not only loses her clan family but, at the time of her husband's death, loses all her material possessions. Her husband's family takes away her belongings and gives them to the husband's nephew.

Daughters remained with their parents until they married and were carefully trained in domestic duties and in ceremonial deportment. At puberty a girl was placed in seclusion where she would have no contact with men. Often a special hut was built for this purpose. During this time a slit was made in her lower lip and a *labret*, a wooden plug, was inserted to enlarge it. The labret is referred to in the story "The Boy Who Shot the Star." A mask with a labret is shown on page 38. Although the practice appalled the early traders and missionaries, to the Tlingit this extended lip was a sign of beauty.

During her seclusion, the young woman was allowed to leave her dwelling only at night. Her only visitors were her mother and her aunts who continued her education in the ways of the people. Her seclusion continued for a period extending anywhere from a few weeks to a year. Young women from high-caste families were kept in seclusion longer than those from lower-caste families. The higher the caste and the longer the seclusion, the purer the young woman. The more "pure" the woman, the higher the bride price that could be demanded from potential suitors and their families. Following this period of separation, a young woman would be married. The aunt and uncle of both the young man and the young woman arranged the marriage. Puberty rites are part of the story "The Mountain Dweller." In this story the girls violate their puberty seclusion and show disregard for other tribal values. Thus, they are banished from the family in shame and told to seek the Mountain Dweller as their husband.

Grandparents had a special place in the lives of children. It was almost impossible for a grandparent to deny anything to a grandchild. This is well demonstrated in the story "Raven Steals the Light." Raven, the trickster, appears in the form of a man's grandchild. The grandchild cries and the grandfather gives the child his sacred trust, the light, and the world is transformed.

Tlingit girl wearing Chilkat blanket and beaded "octopus bag" front piece. (Photograph courtesy of Case and Draper Collection, Alaska State Library, Juneau, Alaska.)

SOCIAL STATUS AND RANK

Many writers report that the Tlingit were divided into three classes: the aristocracy, the commoner, and the slave; however, this is an oversimplification of a complex system of wealth, privilege, and self-esteem. It appears that rather than three classes, there was a range of ranks, from those at the top to the lowliest of slaves (even "slaves" occasionally had slaves). In the stories that follow we have used the distinction provided by Swanton (1909) in describing individuals as high caste or high born. Wealth and social status were admired more than prowess in war and hunting. Hunt and Forman say, "Many societies used wealth as a means of gaining status, but there are few who emphasized it as much as those of the Northwest Coast" (1979, 47). Hunt and Forman go on to explain, however, that the Tlingit concept was not to hoard wealth for oneself, but to accumulate items to be given as gifts. The Tlingits valued the status of showing apparent disregard for material possessions by giving them away. In fact, the gifts were carefully chosen to honor both the receiver and the giver. The more material wealth a person was able to distribute, the higher the status he enjoyed.

Krause reports that not all clans enjoyed the same status. They were "ranked" according to their wealth and numbers. Within the clan the individual families were ranked as well. "They form a sort of aristocracy which bases its position not so much on birth as on the possession of wealth" (1956, 77). The rank of chief is tied up with the possession of wealth, largely the ownership of slaves. The "high born" did not possess any particular privileges except the high esteem in which they were held by their tribespeople. Krause says, "At feasts they are given the places of honor and the richest presents are given them. For the death or injury of an important person greater compensation is demanded than for a person of lesser rank; two or more lives being the payment for one of chief" (1956, 84). Marrying someone of equal rank was very important, and rank determined the gifts that were given at the time of a marriage.

Olson defines status as *face*. He says, "Tlingits put a great emphasis on integrity, honor, bravery and 'face' in social and personal relationships. No insult, wrong, indignity or injury could pass unnoticed or unresolved" (1967, 684). Except for a very few specific crimes, such as witchcraft, most injuries could be mitigated by the payment of reparations of some type.

SLAVES

Wealthier houses kept slaves. Slaves were either prisoners of war, purchased by trade, or offspring of slaves. Although they bore the brunt of the hard labor, they were, in most instances, well treated, with the notable exception of slave sacrifice, which will be discussed later. Their importance was often because of the status they conferred on the owner, since he had to be wealthy in order to support slaves. In fact, they were as great a liability as an asset since their productivity was unlikely to be much greater than the expense of their upkeep. Old Chief Shakes is supposed to have kept more than 70 slaves (Hunt and Forman, 41). Slaves will appear in many of the stories in the second part of the book.

Since slaves were viewed as property, they could be sold or traded. During ceremonies, slaves were often killed to show disregard for the wealth they represented. At the death of a highborn person, slaves were sacrificed so that they might go with the master to serve in the land beyond. At other times, during a joyous occasion, a slave might be set free. Freed slaves lived very much like lower-ranking Tlingits and occasionally married among them.

Ransom figured in preventing certain individuals from becoming slaves. People of high rank were often captured and held for ransom. The reduction of such a person to the status of property (a slave) was a disgrace that could only be removed by the payment of goods. An excessive overpayment removed this stigma more effectively. In "The Story of the Puffin," the father tries to buy his daughter's freedom from her captors with gifts of great value. Wars were occasionally fought for the sole purpose of capturing slaves.

CEREMONIES AND POTLATCHES

The long winter was a time of feasts, which played an important part in the lives of the Tlingit. Feasts were connected with birth and death, successful hunting expeditions, war parties, reconciliation between two quarreling factions, or the raising of a totem pole or a new house.

The most lavish of these parties continued sometimes for days with dancing, sharing of food, and presenting of gifts. A host used careful protocol in selecting both his gifts and his guests. Giving a present that was too extravagant would embarrass the guest, who would not be able to repay the host in kind. On the other hand, a gift that was not equal to the stature and importance of a guest could prove to be a major insult to that person. Krause says, "The apparent generosity of the host, which is contrary to the customary avarice of the Indians, is explained by the fact that at the next opportunity the guests are obliged to give at least the value of the gift in return" (1956, 162). Every aspect of the celebration, from the seating of guests to the serving of food and distribution of presents, was meticulously planned by the host to award both himself and his guests the greatest prestige possible.

These lavish parties have been called *potlatches* in most of the literature about the Tlingits. The term potlatch is derived from the Chinook word *patshatl*, which means "to give away." This party has also been called a payoff or payback party. Many knowledgeable Tlingit people consider both the term potlatch and the definition given to it to be misleading and unauthentic. The Dauenhauers say, "One highly respected Tlingit elder advised us to 'take this word and sink it in the deepest water'" (1990, 36). The general Tlingit term for these celebrations is ḵoo.éex' deriving from the Tlingit verb stem meaning "to call" or "to invite."

The Dauenhauers believe that the real significance of the so-called potlatch was misinterpreted by many non-Tlingit writers and researchers. The Dauenhauers' work gives a Tlingit perspective on this event.

The *memorial potlatch* ideally takes place one year after the death of the one to be honored, but this is flexible. In actual practice today, and no doubt in the past as well, the potlatch may take place years after the person's death because of the time, effort, and expense of hosting such a memorial. Sometimes elders and different families join together to host the memorial, making it for more than one person. Fall was the preferred time for the potlatch because the summer fishing, berry picking, and deer hunting would provide the traditional food for the potlatch. Today, income from commercial fishing provides the needed cash for other gifts.

Tlingit artifacts including Chilkat blanket (at center),
beaded "octopus bag" (upper right), and various ceremonial items in foreground. (Photograph courtesy of
Case and Draper Collection, Alaska State Library,
Juneau, Alaska.)

Tlingit ceremonial articles. Wooden dance hat at left has a woven cylin-
der attached in which eagle down may have been placed. The jerky
movements of the dancer would scatter the sacred down, considered to
be a sign of goodwill. (Photograph courtesy of Elbridge Warren Merrill
Collection, Alaska State Library, Juneau, Alaska.)

The purpose of the memorial potlatch is to provide regard and respect for the dead. The oratory shared is meant to heal. The Dauenhauers say, "Popular understanding and many scholarly treatments have tended to interpret potlatch as a demonstration of wealth and prestige, and have tended to emphasize economic aspects such as the distribution of goods. These aspects are certainly present to some degree in Tlingit memorials, but we feel that there are more important spiritual and healing dimensions that have often been overlooked, ignored or denied" (1990, 38).

The memorial potlatch begins with the ceremony known as *Cry Ceremony.* It is performed by guests from the opposite moiety to remove the grief of the hosts. The Cry Ceremony is very important. The Dauenhauers explain:

> According to traditional Tlingit belief, prolonged grieving is physically and spiritually unhealthy for the community and the individual. Therefore, prolonged grieving for the dead is taboo. The traditional belief is that if sadness lingers over the death of a relative, especially that of matrilineal kin, it will invite the death of another matrilineal kin. It is said that the cries of the relative endanger the life breath of the living. The breath of a family member may flow with the tears.... By crying, the breath of a family member is weakened, thus making him or her vulnerable to death and the spirit world. For this reason, the Cry for the departed is important to all because it formally marks the end of mourning, of crying and of the period of grief (1990, 50).

During the Cry Ceremony the spirits of the departed and other spirits are called through oratory to help remove the grief and give comfort to the living. After the Cry Ceremony is concluded and thanks are given to the guests, the mourning section of the memorial is brought to a close. The atmosphere changes immediately from sorrow to one of gaiety and joy. Songs of mourning are replaced by love songs.

Next the hosts and guests share meals, distribute gifts and money, dance, sing, and listen to more speeches. When gifts such as food and blankets are given for the physical and spiritual warmth of the bereaved, the gifts are believed to pass through the gift receiver and on to the deceased, giving comfort in the spirit world. When all the food, gifts, and money have been distributed, the evening is brought to a joyous close sometimes with a line-dance in which all of the hosts and all of the guests dance together.

The Tlingit culture also contains a type of potlatch known as *sh daatx K̲ux̲'awdligoo* or "wiping the mouth from the body" to address defamation of character. In this type of potlatch, the host tries to, as the Dauenhauers put it, "wipe the slate clean where the individual has been the target of character assassination" (1990, 38). A variation on this theme is the potlatch of reconciliation for wrongs committed. The theme of healing, or feasting with your enemy, is present in the story "The Man Who Entertained the Bears." In the story we also see the importance of oratory at these events.

VALUES

Tlingits have a strong value orientation. Their belief in the rightness and wrongness of things is ever present in their stories. In fact, these stories helped instruct the youth and reinforced values for all as they were shared in the stillness of winter nights. Many values come from their spiritual beliefs; others appear to arise from the culture itself. Spiritual values will be discussed later in this section.

Early explorers and missionaries were impressed with the industry and work ethic of the Tlingit. The hard-working were rewarded; the lazy did not go unpunished. In the beginning of the story "The Orphan," the young woman is rewarded for her industry but later loses her wealth through her lack of compassion for her less fortunate brothers. In "The Man Who Was Abandoned," the main character is left alone to die because he is lazy and therefore worthless. Sometimes the lazy were tolerated but not without difficulty. The mother-in-law in "The Origin of Gonaqadē't, Monster of the Sea" mocks and scorns her son-in-law for his lazy ways, although we find out later in the story that he is a true hero.

The Tlingit believed that all things must be kept in balance. All powers of nature must be treated with courtesy and respect. Nature's gifts must not be exploited and must never be wasted. If persons lived by the rules of nature they were rewarded. If they did not, ill will came to them. In the story "The Salmon Chief," the man does as the Salmon Chief requests, and the man and his wife are rewarded with two sons. The uncle in "The Wolf

Chief's Son" insults his helper and thereby loses this powerful ally. One of the young men in "The Boy Who Shot the Star" does not show proper respect for the moon and he is seized by her and held captive in the sky. The girls in "The Mountain Dweller" take more than they needed and are gluttonous. Thus, they are banished from their family.

Solidarity of clan members is highly valued. We see how horrible it is to be without family in "The Orphan," "The Man Who Was Abandoned," and in "The Man Who Entertained the Bears." Kinship and protection of kin span even death. In "Kushtaka's Captive," an aunt and uncle bring the young man back to the land of the living even though they themselves may never return. In the story "The Sky Country," the man is initially fooled, for he is treated so well that he believes himself to be among his kinsmen. The man in "The Story of the Eagle Crest of the Nexa'di" gives up his life as a human to become an eagle so that he might save his people.

The idea of *face* has been discussed before, and it figures in the context of several of the stories. Face has not only a figurative meaning but a literal meaning as well. Among the Tlingit it was a great insult to cause damage to the face (De Laguna 1972, 175). Should an individual cause damage to another's face, reparations would have to be paid. In "The Mountain Dweller," the mother in her anger does the unthinkable. She scratches the face of one of her daughters. The daughters had sinned grievously, for they had caused their father to lose face or respect. They had eaten up the food that was to be presented to the guests. As the father opened a special box to share delicacies with his guests, he found, to his embarrassment and shame, that the box was empty. So dishonored is the mother-in-law in the story "The Origin of Gonaqadē't, Monster of the Sea," that she closes her door to all and dies in shame.

SPIRITUALISM, RELIGION, AND COSMOLOGY

The early Tlingits were deeply spiritual people; however, they had no consistent set of notions which explained the nature of the world, the natural events that took place in it, or humanity's place in the universe. No cosmological scheme arose from their oral tradition. Uncoordinated sets of myths, however, deal with the origins of certain natural features or human customs. The story of Raven is a tale about the creation of the world as we know it today. While Raven may not have been the creator, he is, nevertheless, a transformer responsible for the current order of things.

The Tlingit people did not worship or believe in a supreme being, nor did they have a system of beliefs that could be called a religion. They did, however, have a deep reverence for the spirituality of all things. As Hunt and Forman say, the Tlingit "shared his world with a profusion of spirits whose presence was reflected in every aspect of his life" (1979, 69). All things possessed power or spiritual force. It was important to respect the spirit of all things and to keep harmony in the environment. Spirits were manifest in different functions. Some spirits, for example, concerned themselves with the everyday lives of people. Others conferred power on the shamans. Still others, particularly animal spirits, gave their special power to ordinary humans.

Animals had spirits of the same basic nature as humans and were able to communicate with them and help them. Tlingit myths abound with stories of animal helpers. In "Little Felon" the main character is helped by a eulachon, a candle fish. "The Man Who Was Abandoned" is saved temporarily by a frog. Spiderwoman, in "The Sky Country," lowers the young couple back to earth. The people are saved from famine by a wolf in "The Wolf Chief's Son" and by an eagle in "The Story of the Eagle Crest of the Nexa'di."

Spirits are everywhere and in everything. The Tlingit believed that proper respect had to be shown, for all words were heard in the omnipresent spirit world. In "The Girl Who Married the Bear," the main character is taken away because she did not show proper respect for the bear. Spirits were both good and evil. The dark side of the spirit world will be explored later.

The Tlingit believed in reincarnation and the transmigration of the spirit. Death was not feared, for they believed that people would be reborn as children of their same clan. Reincarnation could be easily proven. Parents saw the returning spirit in a dream. Often the child was born with a birthmark or other physical characteristic derived from a previous life. De Laguna (1972) said that a person referring to a time before his birth would say, "Then ashes I was; not yet was I born."

It was believed that the dead had to cross a river or lake. Therefore, a euphemism for "he died" was "he went across." In the story "Return from the Spirit Land," the main character must cross a body of water to find his departed wife.

The dead had to be properly cared for or their souls could not return. In traditional Tlingit culture, the dead were cremated because it was believed that the body had to be "warmed up" to release the spirit into the world beyond. Thus, in the story "The Man Who Was Abandoned," even though his family felt that the lazy man was not worthy of their care in life, they still sent their slaves back to give him the proper funeral rites at his death.

Among the Tlingits it was horrible to be drowned. Relatives and friends would search at great length for a person missing in water. Unless the body could be found and cremated, thus releasing the spirit, the departed had to live forever with the underwater spirits. A more feared fate was to be captured by the Kushtaka or Land Otter People. Even today the Tlingits have a special ceremony for drowning victims whose bodies are not recovered to prevent their bodies from being carried off by the Kushtaka.

KUSHTAKA OR LAND OTTER PEOPLE

The Kushtaka has been treated in some literature as a boogeyman or hobgoblin. This is inaccurate and does not honor how seriously the Tlingit feel the threat of the Land Otter People. In a sense, the Kushtaka deprived the victim of everlasting life, for his soul could not be reincarnated. The Land Otter lurked to "save," that is, to capture, those who drowned or who became lost in the woods. The unfortunate captives were taken by the Land Otter People to their homes or dens and, unless rescued by a shaman, were themselves turned into Land Otters. Kushtaka often appeared in the form of relatives or friends to confuse the victim. Dogs were a protection against Land Otter People, for not only were the animals afraid of dogs, but the dogs' barking forced the Land Otter People to reveal themselves. Small children were thought to be the most in danger of being captured by the Land Otter People and were warned not to wander off from parents or to venture away from home alone.

We have included one story about the Kushtaka. In this tale two other beliefs about the Land Otter People also appear. First, a captive does not turn into a Land Otter immediately; the transformation takes place over time. Thus, if he or she is rescued in time, the captive can be redeemed. Second, while Land Otter People are generally considered inimical to human beings, the Kushtaka have been known to help their own relatives.

The Shaman alone with his totem. Note bone spirit catcher in his
left hand, Chilkat blanket and bentwood box in background.
(Photograph courtesy of Case and Draper Collection, Alaska State
Library, Juneau, Alaska.)

THE SHAMAN

The shaman (see color photograph on page 38) was a powerful person in Tlingit society, serving as the interpreter between
the spirits and the people. The shaman was typically male; however, a few female shamans have been reported. Since nearly all
shamans were male, the stories reflect this. The shaman, as
De Laguna reports,

> was the intermediary between men and the
> forces of nature. He cures the sick, controls the
> weather, brings success in war and on the hunt,

foretells the future, communicates with colleagues at a distance, receives news about those who are far away, finds and restores to their families those who are lost and captured by the Land Otter men, reveals and overthrows ... witches and makes public demonstration of his powers in many awe-inspiring ways (1972, 670).

The shaman both controlled and was inspired by supernatural spirits.

The role of shaman was often passed on from a man to his nephew. Sometimes a shaman would be identified at birth by some unusual sign such as a caul, red hair, or crossed eyes. At other times, a child would show a physical likeness to a deceased shaman. Therefore, it was believed that the shaman was reincarnated in the child.

Shaman, whose hair is left long and uncombed, bending over a sick man. He is wearing a ceremonial mask. (Photograph courtesy of Case and Draper Collection, Alaska State Library, Juneau, Alaska.)

To gain power, the shaman went alone into the forest or mountains for a month to a year. There he fasted and tortured himself, hoping that the spirit of an animal would come to him. He hoped especially to see the otter and cut out its tongue, for in the tongue of the otter was said to be the whole secret of shamanism. Since the people had a great respect for that power, the otter was never hunted until the coming of the Russians.

The shaman used ceremonial objects such as masks, rattles, drums, and soul catchers. These were passed on to a relative at the time of the shaman's death.

Two of the stories in the book deal in some degree with shamanism. In "The Image That Came to Life," the loving husband calls the shaman to save his failing wife. In another, "The Origin of Gonaqadē't, Monster of the Sea," the mother-in-law decides that she is a powerful shaman who can command the food-gathering spirits. She demands that her husband create ceremonial objects for her.

One of the shaman's major responsibilities was to cure the sick. Sickness was not generally viewed as part of the natural order by the Tlingit. In most cases they believed that illness was caused by the malicious intent of a malevolent person referred to as a witch. Part of the shaman's responsibility was to divine the witch's identity and then force the witch to confess and to remove the "curse."

WITCHCRAFT

Some Tlingits are embarrassed by references to witchcraft. Many cultures—early American, European, Asian, and African—had witches. It would be odd if the Tlingits did not also share this almost universal belief in these malevolent persons.

The witch, or "master of sickness," was the most despised human being in the Tlingit culture. De Laguna says,

> The witch was feared and loathed because there was no antisocial, evil or unnatural act of which he was not believed capable: dishonesty, shamelessness, incest, mysterious powers of locomotion or bodily transformation, and above all, corroding spite and jealousy that made him cause the illness or death of those he envied (1972, 728).

Oberg observed that among the Tlingits only two crimes were punishable by death: witchcraft and incest (1973, 129).

Most witches were thought to act upon their victim by obtaining a piece of clothing, hair, or spittle from the person. The witch would then make an image of the person and treat it whatever way the witch wanted the person to suffer. A witch seemed controlled by his or her own evil power, helpless to resist injuring others. Only through a confession after torture could the witch be released and the victim rescued. An in-depth review of witchcraft beliefs among the Tlingit can be found beginning on page 728 of the De Laguna study.

We have included several stories that include elements of witchcraft. In "The Faithless Wife," a man plays with the bones of the dead so that he may obtain the power of a witch and destroy his faithless wife and her lover. A jealous woman in "The Woman Who Married the Dead Man" "witches" the two returning hunters by spreading blood on their seats and thereby dooms them to return to the land of the dead. In "The Man Who Entertained the Bears," the man is afraid to seek out new companions after the death of all of the members of his clan because he fears that he will be accused of witchcraft. A jealous suitor in "Return from the Spirit Land" causes the death of the husband and thereby banishes both the husband and wife to the spirit land.

Tlingit belief in the power of the shaman seriously eroded during the smallpox epidemic of 1836, which is reported to have killed half of the native population while taking only one Russian life. The smallpox vaccine saved the Russians and convinced some Tlingits of the superior knowledge of the Russians. With their faith destroyed in their own shamans, some Tlingits began to convert to Christianity.

Art and Art Forms

Abundant food in their homeland gave the Tlingits the leisure to develop the beautiful, complex art forms still enjoyed today. Imagine how the Europeans felt when they sailed into a bay and saw the forty-foot totem poles with their strange and complex symbolism. They might have thought they were entering the garden of some ancient and long forgotten gods. Or imagine their puzzlement when they examined the strongly woven spruce root baskets so finely crafted that they were watertight and could be used as cooking vessels. Think of how they felt when they ran their fingers across a bentwood box constructed from a single piece of wood gently steamed and bent into a box. Who were these people who carved their canoes with the same quality that Europeans carved their statues?

The Tlingit were exceptional craftspeople. Theirs was mostly an applied and decorative art. They created beautiful, functional items from common materials: wood, shell, bone, roots and grasses, stone, animal hides, and metal. Even everyday objects such as fishhooks and serving spoons were deftly crafted and adorned in the distinctive style of the northwest coast.

THE DESIGN

Even the untutored observer recognizes the important role that symbolism plays in the art of northwest coast Indians. Tlingit two-dimensional art is not realistic in the ordinary sense. Leonhard Adam describes the distinct principles of the art, which include: (1) stylized as opposed to realistic representation, (2) schematic characterization that accentuates certain features, (3) splitting, (4) dislocating split details, (5) representing one creature by two profiles, (6) symmetry (with exceptions), (7) reducing, and (8) illogical transformation of details into new representations (Holm 1965, 8). The representation of various animals will be described in more detail in the totem section.

All Tlingit painting and carving is characterized by the use of two basic formlines: the ovoid and the U. The ovoid has been called a rounded rectangle, an angular oval, and a bean-shaped figure. The ovoid formline is used as eyes, joints, and various space fillers. The U form results when both ends of a formline turn in the same direction, and each end tapers to a point as it meets another formline. The primary formlines merge and connect to form a smoothly flowing, continuous design, usually black in color.

Many books have been written to explain this complex art form in detail. Such a discussion is beyond the scope of this book; however, the authors recommend several books in the bibliography, particularly Bill Holm's *Northwest Coast Indian Art: An Analysis of Form* (1989).

COLOR

Color is another unifying element in northwest coast art. Black, red, and blue-green are the colors most frequently used. The main formlines of the design are generally black. Red accents lips, cheeks, and tongues, and occasionally the hands and feet. Blue-green is used to fill in eye sockets and other small spaces. The colors are created from natural materials so the amount and color used is dependent on the availability of the natural resources of the area.

TOTEM POLES

Towering above the plank houses, or occasionally constructed as part of them, is the art form that has stimulated the imagination of explorers of southeastern Alaska, both in times long past and today.

The totem, like most Tlingit artwork, is functional as well as decorative. Early Russian missionaries mistakenly believed that the totem pole was an object of worship or idolatry. Several of these magnificent monuments were burned by zealous Christians who did not understand their true purpose.

Totems generally fall into one of several categories:

- house pillars
- mortuary or funeral poles

- heraldic portals or family poles
- shame or ridicule poles
- memorial poles

The house pillar served as a support for the building beams in the clan house. Early house posts were carved from one piece of wood. Later, some carvings were done on a separate slab of wood and then attached to the pole.

Mortuary poles were repositories for the remains of the dead. Early poles were simple. The ashes of a cremated person were placed in a box at the top of a plain pole. Later the poles had one main carving at the top, with the deceased's remains buried in the ground behind the pole or placed in a hollowed-out section of the pole. As Christianity spread throughout Alaska in the 1800s, the practice of cremating the dead and erecting mortuary poles was abandoned in favor of burial. Few examples of this type of pole exist today except in museums.

The heraldic portal or the family pole framed the entrance to the Tlingit clan house. Figures reflecting the family's crest were carved on the pole. The actual entryway, or the negative space, was part of the totemic design.

The shame or ridicule pole was commissioned to force the payment of a debt by publicly humiliating the debtor. This form of public ridicule was used only after all other diplomatic means of settling the debt had failed. Battles were fought over such loss of face. The debtor's deeds were illustrated in graphic form. Often the shamed one's crest was carved upside down as a way of embarrassing him. White traders who bartered unfairly with the Tlingits were sometimes portrayed this way. When the debt was paid, the debtor's family was allowed to burn the ridicule pole as a tangible way of showing that the score was settled. A person might also be ridiculed by forcing him to cut several feet off his totem pole, thereby reducing both the totem and its owner in stature and favor with the clan.

Memorial poles were of great significance in the Tlingit culture. When an important person died, a carver from the opposite moiety was employed to create a pole commemorating that person's life. The dedication of the pole, usually one year after the death, was cause for great celebration.

Red cedar, beautiful and soft enough to carve easily, was the preferred wood of carvers. Its odor repelled insects naturally, giving it a longer life than other types of wood. Where red cedar did not grow, such as around Sitka and areas north, carvers would sometimes make dangerous journeys by canoe to select a log and tow it back to their site. Yellow cedar or Sitka spruce was sometimes used as a substitute for the red cedar.

The carver usually was a commissioned artist, who made preliminary sketches of each section of the pole. Each of these was approved by the chief before the work was begun. Carvers used some creative license in their design, and each developed his own unique style of carving, while adhering to traditional guidelines of the art form.

Clan crests were the property of that clan. A carver of the Bear clan, for example, would never work on a Wolf motif without a commission from a member of that clan. To do so would be a breach of etiquette and would invite serious repercussions from the clan whose property rights were violated.

Totem poles were not actually "read," as some people might believe. Rather, the figures and motifs carved on them suggested stories that only the carver and the person who commissioned the pole understood until the unveiling ceremony. Then, with song, dance, and story, the totem's meaning was revealed.

A pole afforded limited carving area. Figures were sometimes combined or carved overlapping one another, but not merely to save room. The placement of figures or parts of images within the design all contributed significantly to the meaning of the totem's story.

Totem carvings had standard features. Human figures had ears carved on the sides. If the ears rose directly over the forehead the form was a mammal or a bird. When women appeared on the pole, they were distinguished from men by the labret in their lower lips.

Raven had a straight beak and lifelike wings. Occasionally he was painted black and had some human features. He was sometimes shown with the motifs that identified him with his famous legends such as the moon and the sun. Raven was distinguished from Eagle, who had heavy claws, a white head, and a downturned beak.

Bear was sometimes confused with Wolf. Both had long snouts and sharp teeth, although Bear did not have a tail. Wolf had pointed ears, which slanted back, and a bushy tail. Occasionally he was shown with a long, lolling tongue.

Whale had a protruding fin, which was carved separately and then attached with a wooden dowel or with glue made from boiled halibut fins. Beaver had large front teeth and a paddle-shaped tail with a cross-hatch design on it. He was often seen holding a stick between his front paws.

A suggestion of Octopus was made by carving one or more tentacles, showing the suckers underneath. These suckers were sometimes further stylized, appearing as faces.

Paint accentuated important details of the figures, such as the eyes, mouths, ears, fins, and wings. Crushed salmon eggs provided the base for the paint and were mixed with various pigments—iron oxides for red, copper-stained clay for blue-green, and charcoal for black.

For all the work put into creating a totem pole, which might take months or even years, very little effort was expended in preserving these wooden monuments. The damp climate and moist spongy earth would usually rot the base of the totem in fewer than 75 years. Then the magnificent monument would decay, returning to the rainforest from which it came.

SPRUCE ROOT BASKETRY

Although no one can pinpoint exactly when the craft of basketry (see color photograph on page 39) came to Alaska, Tlingit folklore says that the first basket originated near Yakutat, located in the northern end of the Alaska panhandle.

> Many years ago, in the time when Raven still walked among men, bringing good to his creatures in strange and inexplicable ways, a woman lived in the cloud country with her beautiful daughter. They were taken there from Earth by Raven, who possessed mysterious powers of the spirit in those days.

> This girl was greatly desired by mortal men as a wife, and many of them made the dangerous journey to the village to consort with her. The young suitors enticed her with descriptions of the majestic mountains, whispering rainforests, and beautiful inlets in their world. Although their sweet words stirred a great longing in the young woman's heart for her homeland, she refused each of the handsome men. They had to return to the Earth, dejected and disappointed.

> It happened that the Sun, Ga-gahn, on one of his trips across the Sky World, chanced to look upon the beautiful maiden. His heart was full of desire for her, and he wished to make her

his bride. At the end of his day's journey, Ga-gahn transformed himself into a man and sought the girl, who consented to mate with him.

As time went on, she bore him many children, and they lived happily together among the clouds. But the children were of the Earth World, like their mother, and not of the Spirit World, like their father, Ga-gahn. As the woman watched her children romping and playing in the fields of the Sky Country, she felt sad that they would never dabble their bare toes in a clear, cold mountain stream, nor pick ripe, plump salmonberries by the handful. As she fretted thus about their future, the woman plucked some roots and began to plait them idly into the shape of a basket. Her husband, the Sun, being of the Spirit World, understood her distress. He took the basket which she had woven and made it large enough to hold her and all eight of their children. As they settled into the vessel, he lowered them gently to Earth, where they came to rest near Yakutat on the Alsek River. That is why the first baskets in southeast Alaska were made by Yakutat women.

(Adapted from *The Legend of the Origin of Basketry* by Frances Paul)

A young girl learns the craft of spruce root basketry by watching an experienced weaver at work. (Photograph courtesy of the Case and Draper Collection, Alaska State Library, Juneau, Alaska.)

Spruce root baskets. Note the three-banded design on all of the baskets. Basket at upper left has a triangular pattern below the bottom band, called a "descender." (Photograph courtesy of Elbridge Warren Merrill Collection, Alaska State Library, Juneau, Alaska.)

Spruce root baskets varied greatly in size, shape, design, and purpose. The largest of these baskets could hold up to 25 gallons of oil; the smallest may have been used to carry an ounce of tobacco. Many baskets were so ingeniously woven that they were watertight and could even be used as cooking vessels. Hot stones dropped into a basket containing water, meat, or berries produced steam and cooked the food under a tight-fitting cover.

The gathering of materials and weaving of baskets was traditionally a female task. All women learned to make baskets. Young girls learned the craft while sitting at the side of a female relative, watching carefully as the elder woman deftly wove the strands of spruce root. At the age of 6 or 7, a girl attempted her first basket, which was expected to be perfect in form and in weaving technique. If her teacher spied a mistake even several rows back in the weaving, she would likely rip out all the work to that point and have her young pupil begin again. In this way girls learned patience and perseverance and the importance of doing a task correctly the first time.

Spruce roots were gathered and prepared in the spring. An experienced woman selected a mature Sitka spruce tree, judging the tree by its size and location. She looked for a site where only spruce trees grew rather than a mixed stand of hemlock, cedar, alder, and spruce. The woman and her female helpers used digging sticks to prod for roots. When a root was found, it was carefully traced from its origin to its end, which might be a distance of 20 to 30 feet. The roots were then cut, coiled, and set aside for the next step.

Within 24 hours, before the sap had a chance to dry, the roots had to be prepared. Basketmakers steamed coils of root over a bed of coals to loosen the outer bark. The bark was then stripped off by pulling each root strand through a split stick called an *eena.*

The next step in the process was to split the root down the middle and to remove the heart, or pith, of the root, which was then discarded. After that basketmakers divided the root into strands again.

Different parts of the root were valued for properties that made them suitable for different parts of the basket. The outside strands, because of their luster, were saved for the weft, the horizontal strands of the basket. The slightly tougher part of the root was used for the warp, or vertical splints.

Basketmakers developed a technique known as "false embroidery" for decorating their baskets. Grasses were dyed, using natural materials, and were wrapped around the weft strand in geometric patterns so that the design only showed on the outside of the basket. Weavers mentally calculated these complex design configurations with precision to create perfectly symmetrical baskets.

Baskets created between 1800 and 1900 commonly appeared with a three-banded design. Out of approximately fifty traditional design patterns, a woman might only master five or six, so her weaving gradually developed a distinctive style. Intermarriage between moieties helped spread these designs throughout southeast Alaska as women shared their knowledge with their new relatives.

Around the turn of the century white traders began to influence the craft of basketry. They encouraged Tlingit women to weave baskets for sale. For the first time, nongeometric designs, such as animals, began to appear on the baskets. Weavers now had access to commercially purchased dyes also, which made the process of decorating the baskets less tedious. Baskets, once a necessity in Tlingit culture, became more of a trade item as other types of vessels became available to women for cooking and storage.

BENTWOOD BOXES

These ingeniously made boxes (see color photograph on page 39) were crafted from a single slab of wood split from a red cedar tree. Woodcrafters evened the slab along the sides and surface using handmade tools of bone and wood. They cut three grooves across the grain of the wood to bend the slab without splitting it. A shallow trench was dug and filled with water, which was heated to steaming by hot stones. Laid across the trench and covered with seaweed, each groove in the plank was steamed in turn. Then woodcrafters bent the plank along each groove, forming the box. The sides and bottom of the box were pegged with handhewn wooden dowels or, occasionally, sewn with cedar root. If the box was used for an important ceremonial purpose, such as the box mentioned in "The Mountain Dweller," it may have been inlaid with abalone or dentalia shells and was probably painted with the owner's clan crest.

COSTUME

Tlingit female artisans were well known for their decorative regalia. The *chilkat* dance blankets were particularly worthy of note (see color photograph on page 40). Mountain goat wool, dyed with the natural materials in traditional black, white, yellow, and blue, was supplemented with shredded cedar bark in the weaving process. The cedar bark strengthened the blanket's fibers and provided the characteristic drape about the body of the dancer. The weavers used a standardized system for the placement of colors in the pattern.

White traders introduced woolen blankets into the culture, primarily from the Hudson's Bay Company. These were used throughout the nineteenth century to make a new style of dance blanket, the appliqued button blanket. The blankets were made from red, navy blue, or black wool. A person's clan crest was appliqued on a rectangular piece of wool and outlined with buttons. Sometimes as many as 1,500 buttons were painstakingly sewn on one blanket. This type of design also appeared on shirts, dance aprons, and leggings.

Chilkat blanket woven in the Killer Whale design. (Photograph courtesy of the Elbridge Warren Merrill Collection, Alaska State Library, Juneau, Alaska.)

European and Russian trade also introduced another innovation in costume design. The Tlingit exchanged sea otter pelts for tiny glass beads of different colors. Women embellished their regalia in complex patterns of light-catching glass. Color photographs of costumes, a ceremonial octopus bag, and a feasting bowl appear on pages 41 and 42.

CONCLUSION

We have explored in this part much of what makes the Tlingits who they are: their land, climate, history, kinship structure, values, religion, and art. In part 2, the reader will see the Tlingit through the rich texture of their myths and legends. Through the people, we know the stories, and the stories teach about the people.

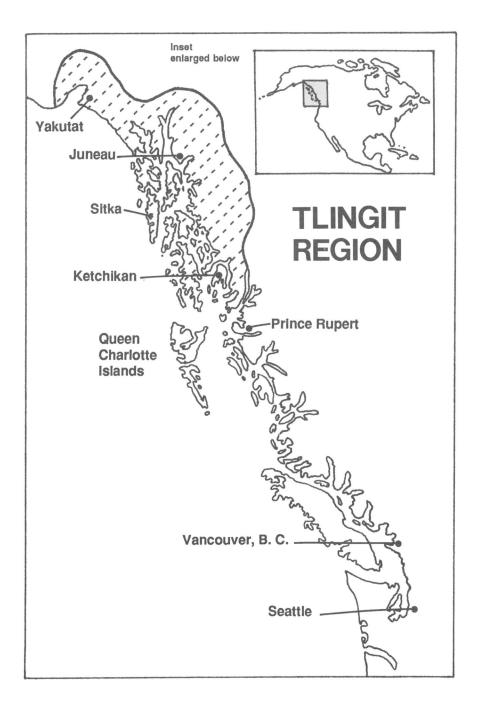

Inset enlarged below

TLINGIT REGION

Yakutat

Juneau

Sitka

Ketchikan

Prince Rupert

Queen Charlotte Islands

Vancouver, B. C.

Seattle

Color Photographs

Color Photographs

The Bicentennial Totem Pole stands in front of the National Park Service Building in Sitka National Historical Park, Sitka, Alaska. (Photograph by Mary Helen Pelton.)

Close-up of one section of the Bicentennial Totem Pole, located in Sitka National Historical Park, showing Raven, on the left, carved with straight beak, and Eagle, at right, with curved beak.

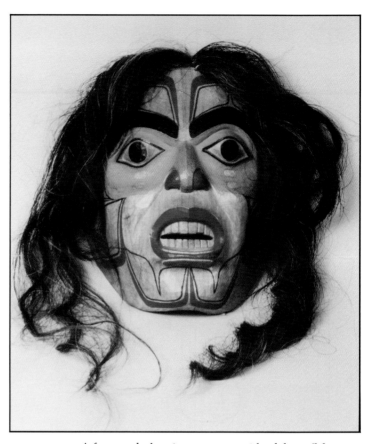

A face mask showing a woman with a labret. (Museum catalog number I.A. 249. Photograph courtesy of the Sheldon Jackson Museum, Sitka, Alaska. Photograph by Ernest Manewal.)

This shaman figure was used in a contest between shamans in 1888. The figure holds a curved stick in each hand with a dew claw of a deer hanging from it. (Museum catalog number I.A. 34. Photograph courtesy of the Sheldon Jackson Museum, Sitka, Alaska. Photograph by Ernest Manewal.)

This spruce root basket has two wide bands of green and red dyed spruce root with a narrow band of red, yellow, and black. (Museum catalog number I.A. 118. Photograph courtesy of the Sheldon Jackson Museum, Sitka, Alaska.)

This bentwood box is made from a single plank of cedar steamed, bent, and sewed with spruce root. The box is painted blue, red, and black. The sides of the cover are decorated with opercula (shell covering) of the sea snail. (Museum catalog number I.A. 1 a,b. Photograph courtesy of the Sheldon Jackson Museum, Sitka, Alaska. Photograph by Ernest Manewal.)

This herring rock blanket was used as a robe on ceremonial occasions by one of the Kiksadi Clan. It depicts the Sitka legend of the Herring Rock. Chilkat blankets such as this were made from mountain goat wool and cedar bark and required about a year to weave. (Photograph courtesy of Sitka National Historical Park, Sitka, Alaska.)

The ceremonial dance shirt has a beaded design of the Wolf crest on the front and includes a multicolored floral design. (Museum catalog number I.A. 463. Photograph courtesy of the Sheldon Jackson Museum, Sitka, Alaska. Photograph by Ernest Manewal.)

The button blanket, carved frontlet headdress, and ceremonial shirt are part of the costuming of the Tlingit. The headdress has a wolf head carved into the frontlet with shells and teeth set in the mouth and abalone shells around the outside. The shirt has the designs of Mt. St. Elias, the Spirit of the Mountain, and the North Wind on the front. (Museum catalog number I.A. 324. Photograph courtesy of the Sheldon Jackson Museum, Sitka, Alaska. Photograph by Stephen E. Hilson.)

After the Russians came to the land of the Tlingit, the native people traded for cloth and glass beads. This octopus bag was made from red felt and is decorated with floral and scroll beadwork. (Museum catalog number I.A. 282. Photograph courtesy of Sheldon Jackson Museum, Sitka, Alaska. Photograph by Ernest Manewal.)

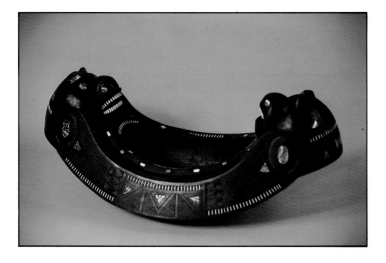

This feasting bowl is elaborately designed with bear heads at the ends. The bowl is carved in one piece and has abalone and bone insets. (Museum catalog number I.A. 272. Photograph courtesy of the Sheldon Jackson Museum, Sitka, Alaska. Photograph by Ernest Manewal.)

Sunset paints a rosy blush on Mt. Edgecumbe volcano. Legend has it that the Tlingit once lived on Kruzof Island, in the shadow of "Shee," or "Lady of the Mountain," as they called the volcano. The Tlingit clans took the name of "Shee Atiká," after her. (Photograph by Dan Evans.)

Tufted puffins make their home on St. Lazaria Island, near Sitka. Note legend of the Puffin Chief on page 57, which explains "how the puffin got its tuft." (Photograph by Dan Evans.)

Snow-capped mountains plunge dramatically to meet the sea in a panorama characteristic of southeast Alaska. (Photograph by Jim DiGennaro.)

Ferns and other flora abound in the organic soil and moist climate of southeast Alaska, which boasts an annual rainfall of nearly 100 inches. (Photograph by Dan Evans.)

The Creation and Why Things Came to Be

The myths speak to our common and ancient roots; they bind us culture to culture into a family of humankind.

Raven Steals the Light

Long ago, so many years ago that, even among the elders, none can remember this time, there was no light in the world. People found their way from place to place by listening carefully to the sounds their footsteps made as they picked their way along a trail. They noticed the soft feel of pine needles beneath their feet and listened to the sigh of wind in the hemlock trees as they reached a certain point in their journey. With their fingers the people carved grooves in the trees along a path. In this way they could remember where to turn going to the spring for water or to the house of a friend.

Story collected from Katishan, chief of the Kasqague′di. Recorded in Wrangell, Alaska. Story adapted for this collection.

The light from the sun, the moon, and the stars was held captive by an old man, who lived at the head of the Nass River. No one, not even his beloved daughter, was allowed to take the light from the boxes where he had hidden it. So his daughter, like all the other people of the village, had to grope her way to the spring to find water for cooking.

Raven, the trickster, was tired of living in darkness. He could not see the beauty of the world around him, and in his vanity, he felt sad that no one could see and admire his great beauty and his magnificent plumage. Raven was determined to find a way to bring light into the world from its hiding place in the old man's house.

First, Raven turned himself into a speck of dirt and hid in the basket the old man's daughter used to collect fresh water. He thought that in this way he could trick her into swallowing him.

As the girl dipped her basket into the spring, however, she murmured to herself, "I don't remember if I cleaned this basket yesterday. I had better throw this water away and collect some more." So Raven was dashed to the ground with the water, where his feelings, as well as his feathers, were very much ruffled.

Next, Raven changed himself into a single hemlock needle and attached himself to a branch along the path where the old man's daughter groped her way to the spring each day. As her fingers brushed against the bough where Raven was attached, the hemlock needle broke loose and drifted down into the young girl's basket. This time, as she dipped her basket into the spring, the hemlock needle floated gently on the surface of the water, where it remained as she carried it home.

When the girl paused for a drink of the cool water from her basket, the Raven-turned-hemlock-needle slipped unnoticed down her throat and into her belly, where it began to grow into a boy-child.

The time came for the girl to deliver, and a hole was dug in which she would give birth in the usual Tlingit manner. Although the birthing place was comfortably lined with soft furs, the baby would not come forth, for he did not want to be born on these fine furs. His grandfather had the furs removed and soft moss put in their place, and then the baby was born.

The baby's eyes darted all around, trying to pierce the darkness. Somewhere beneath night's heavy black blanket were the boxes containing the light. His soft baby croon, like the bubbly warble that Raven can make, enchanted his grandfather, who delighted in holding the child. But the baby could also wail with the hoarse, raucous cry of Raven. During these times the grandfather was beside himself trying to quiet the young boy.

As the baby grew he began to crawl and to explore the house where he lived with his mother and grandfather. The grandfather, like all grandfathers before him and since, indulged his young grandchild. He made rattles for the boy from dried deer hooves, which he fastened to a stick. This amused the Raven-child for a time, until he discovered the light-boxes hidden in the corner. The child pointed at the boxes and wailed piteously until his grandfather could stand the awful sound no longer.

"Give my grandson what he is crying for!" insisted the old man to his daughter. "Give him that small box in the corner."

So the Raven-child was given the smallest of the boxes, which contained the stars. He chortled and crooned his melodious Raven cry as he rolled the stars about on the floor. Suddenly, he tossed them high in the air, through the smokehole. The stars continued heavenward, scattering themselves about the sky, where they remain until this day. Then the boy began to cry again, louder and harsher than before, all the while pointing to the boxes that were hidden away.

"Let him play with the moon, then," said the grandfather, holding his hands over his ears to shut out the racket.

He handed the medium-sized box to the child to open. The boy was delighted, rolling and bouncing the beautiful, luminous ball around and around the house. He played catch with his mother, his black eyes dancing with mischief as they were illuminated by the silvery light. All at once he bounced the moon hard against the floor. It flew high over his mother's head and out of the smokehole, coming to rest at last in the topmost branches of a tall spruce tree.

Raven-child's gurgles of delight soon turned to hideous wails of dismay as he begged once more for the remaining prize in the corner. There was nothing his grandfather or mother could do to console him except to give him the last and largest of the boxes.

When the boy opened this box, which contained the daylight, he gave the Raven cry "Ga." Then, changing himself into his true raven form, he flew up through the smokehole with the light. The grandfather and his daughter had just enough time to catch a glimpse of Raven in his magnificent plumage before he was gone, streaking across the sky with the light that he had released from the box.

As for the daughter, she was delighted that she no longer had to grope her way to the spring for water. And after that, she always looked in her basket for any stray hemlock needles before she drank.

Origin of the Killer Whale

A man named Nātsalane', of the Seal people, enjoyed carving killer whales. First he tried to carve them out of red cedar, but the wood's pungent fragrance made him dreamy and stupid, and his knife slipped and cut his hand deeply. Next he tried hemlock, but the shaggy bark was tough and hard to peel, and he abandoned his effort when he was only half finished with the figure. Nātsalane' then attempted to fashion a killer whale from the wood of

Story collected from Katishan, chief of the Kasqague'di. Recorded in Wrangell, Alaska. Story adapted for this collection.

the Sitka spruce, but the wood was too green and split badly. He took his crude figures to the beach and tried to make them swim out, but each one floated up to the surface. Finally Nātsalane' took the wood of the yellow cedar, which was perfect for carving, and he created several killer-whale figures.

He designed each of these uniquely. On one he marked white lines with Indian chalk from the corners of its mouth back to its head.

Nātsalane' said, "This is going to be the white-mouthed killer whale." Another one he shaped long and slender, and he named it *Kit-wusā'ni* or "killer-whale-spear."

When he first put them into the water, he headed them up the inlet, telling them that whenever they went up to the heads of the bays they were to hunt for seal, halibut, and all the other things that live in the sea, but they were not to hurt a human being.

In those days it was a secret among the killer whales that they could leave the seas and go ashore like human beings to camp. The killer-whale chief and his party were encamped when a man and his wife paddled by on their way to a certain bay to catch halibut. Time after time they cast their halibut hook and line into the water, but they had no luck catching fish. Finally, hungry and discouraged, the two decided to quit for the day. Just then the man felt a pull on his line and saw the silver flash of a halibut. As he pulled it in, however, a shark swam up to the surface, cut his line with its sharp teeth, and carried off both the hook and the fish. Now the man and his wife had no means to catch fish, so they started to paddle homeward.

As the humans went along they saw a campfire blazing on the beach, and they paddled closer, thinking that there were people on the shore.

When the human beings drew close, the killer-whale chief cried, "I feel people staring at us! Quickly, jump into the ocean and swim away!"

The man and his wife landed the canoe and went up to the killer whales' camp. There they found an abundance of food from the sea: salmon, halibut, abalone, and seal. The man's wife said, "It is lucky for us that we found this! I will fill my cooking basket with water and we will have a feast."

As she was dipping her basket into the water, the woman looked out on the sea. Shading her eyes with her hand, she said, "I see a canoe coming way out on the water. We had better leave our meal until the canoe comes so we can invite them to eat with us."

By now the man was also peering out across the water. "I do not think that is a canoe," he replied, "it is much too black."

The long black shape was really a young killer whale carried on the backs of the other killer whales to make it appear like a canoe. When they reached the shore, they rose up thick and black and snatched the woman from behind her husband's back where she was trying to hide. They carried her to the water because they were so angry at her for stealing their provisions and dove into the bay, swimming away as fast as they could.

When the killer whales came to a place opposite a high cliff where the water was deep, they suddenly dived down into the sea, out of sight. Keeping in sight the spot where the whales disappeared from view, the man climbed the cliff. He fastened a slim spruce bough to his head, another around his waist, and filled his shirt with rocks. Then he jumped into the sea at the place where his wife had disappeared.

He sank deep into the water until at last he reached the bottom of the ocean. The man began walking along the bottom until he came to a long row of houses belonging to the shark people. Entering the last house, he spotted a man with a crooked mouth peering at him from behind a post. The one who peered at him was really the hook that the shark had carried off.

The man with the crooked mouth said, "Master, it is I, your hook. When the shark people broke your line, they brought me down here and made me their slave."

"What news do you have of my wife who was taken captive by the killer whales?" the man asked.

The hook replied, "Right across from us is the killer whales' town. Recently I heard that a woman had been captured there and is now married to the killer-whale chief."

The man cried, "How can I rescue my wife and bring her back to the world of the human beings?"

"Listen carefully, Master," replied the hook. "The killer-whale chief has a slave who is always chopping wood in the forest with a stone axe. When you come to him, say softly to yourself, 'I wish his axe would break.' Wish it continually." The hook went on, outlining a plan to save the man's wife from the killer whales.

The man went over to the killer-whale town as the halibut hook had instructed. There he found the slave with the axe, cutting wood for the evening fire. As the slave swung the axe down time and time again, the man did as he was instructed. Over and over he chanted, "I wish his axe would break, I wish his axe would break." The tree strained and split as one blow after another fell on her ruptured skin. Then the slave raised the axe high and the next blow was his last. The axe broke in two.

The man stepped out of the shadows and said to the slave, "I will help you to fix that axe if only you will tell me where my wife is being kept." The slave was happy to comply as his axe was the only one in the whole killer-whale town, and he did not know how to fix it himself.

When the axe was repaired, the slave led the man to the house where the woman was kept. The man waited outside until the evening fire was lit in the house. Then he rushed in and threw a great quantity of water on the fire. As the steam rose up from the fire, the man grabbed his wife and dashed out of the lodge. Although he could not see in the boiling mist, he could hear his halibut hook shouting, "This way, Master! This way!"

As the mist cleared, the killer whales saw that their prized captive had been taken away. They searched in all directions but could see no sign of the man, the wife, or the hook.

The chief of the killer whales cried, "It is the sharks that have taken her. We'll teach them to take what belongs to us."

With that they attacked the sharks. The sharks swam out to some rocks and sharpened their teeth into deadly points. Then they returned the attack, ripping open the soft underbellies of the killer whales with their teeth. While the battle raged, the man and the woman followed the halibut hook to safety, back to the world of the human beings.

All of this happened a long time ago. Much has changed in the world since that time. The killer whales can no longer come to shore and assume human form nor can people live beneath the sea. But some things will never change. Even today when the shark people meet the killer-whale people in the bay, they fight to the death. And the people of the earth still tremble if they find themselves near the battlefield of these great warriors, for who knows when they both might turn on man, their mutual enemy?

The Story of the Puffin

There were some young women in a village whose habit it was to paddle to a nearby island at low tide to gather shellfish. The women always paddled their canoe by the same route, which took them past a hole in the side of the island where a flock of puffins nested.

The youngest woman would gaze fondly at the beautiful birds and say to the others, "I wish I could sit among them, even for a moment."

One day, as the women approached the island, a sudden swell rose from the sea and upset their canoe. The women cried piteously for help, but the only voice heard by the puffin chief above the crash of the waves was that of the youngest woman. He sent his puffin flock to rescue the woman and bring her back to the island.

Meanwhile, back in the village, drum beats called people to the death feast. The villagers believed the young women had drowned.

After several days the youngest woman's father paddled in a canoe past the place where the puffins nested. The man looked up and saw his daughter sitting among the birds. At first he hardly recognized her, for although her body was familiar and humanlike, in place of her nose she had a colorful orange beak like the puffins. The man rejoiced to find his daughter alive and was determined to get her back before she was completely transformed into one of the birds.

Story collected from an elder of the Box-house people, DeKinā′k, in Sitka, Alaska. Story adapted for this collection.

Since he was very wealthy, the man loaded a canoe with sea otter, beaver, and marten skins, thinking that he would trade the beautiful skins for his daughter. Although he paddled past the place day after day, the puffins refused to fly out to his canoe. Dejected, the man returned home to his wife. The girl's mother had an idea. "Remember the white hair that belonged to my grandfather?" she asked. "I still keep it in a box. Let's make a plan to trade the hair for our daughter."

The man placed a board across the gunwales of his canoe and carefully spread the grandfather's hair on the board. Then once again he paddled out to where the puffins nested. This time several of the birds flew out from the hole in the island and circled above his canoe, calling noisily to one another before flying back to their chief to tell him about the hair.

They pressed the puffin chief to trade the girl for the beautiful white hair. Reluctantly, he sent several of his flock to carry the young woman back to her father.

Before she left he said, "If you are ever unhappy living among the human beings, you can always come back to live with us."

The puffins dropped her gently into the canoe with her father. Then, as each bird swooped down past the canoe, the girl stuck a tuft of white hair on its head.

Today, all puffins from the island still sport a tuft of white hair on their heads. And unfortunately for the young woman who admired the beautiful birds, she, too, still has the bright orange beak of a puffin.

Beaver and Porcupine

$\mathbb{A}$ beaver and a porcupine were once the best of friends. They would travel everywhere together, exploring the woods and shoreline. Often the porcupine would visit his friend beaver at his dam on the river. On these occasions, the porcupine would sometimes leave behind several sharp quills by accident as he brushed against the sides of the lodge.

"Ouch!" the beaver would cry when his round, fat body came in contact with the wicked barbs. "Can't you be more careful?"

The beaver would then have to sit back on his haunches, irritated and grouchy, while the porcupine gently removed the quills with his teeth. But in spite of the inconvenience of an occasional quill in the backside, the beaver truly enjoyed having his friend porcupine visit him in his home on the lake.

All beavers had one fearsome enemy, bear, who liked nothing better than to break up the animals' dams, draining the water. Then the bear would catch the beavers and eat them. The bear, however, was afraid of porcupines, for he had come into contact with their painful quills on more than one occasion. So when porcupine was in the lodge visiting beaver, the little animal knew he was safe from his enemy, bear.

One day beaver and porcupine were enjoying a friendly conversation inside beaver's warm, dry lodge when they noticed the water level falling rapidly.

"It is bear!" cried beaver fearfully.

Story collected from an elder of the Box-house people, Dekináʼk, in Sitka, Alaska. Story adapted for this collection.

"Wait here," said his friend. "I will go outside and see what is causing the problem."

Sure enough, as porcupine poked his head out of the lodge, he spotted bear quite close by, waiting for his prey to come out so he could catch him and eat him. When bear saw porcupine, he backed cautiously away and sat at some distance watching, for he wanted to avoid the painful barbs of the spiky animal.

Then porcupine called to his friend to come outside, and he stood guard while beaver repaired his dam. Tired of waiting for his supper, bear lumbered back into the woods, and beaver was safe once again.

After a while porcupine began to get hungry and wanted to return to his own house in the woods. Porcupine got his food from the bark and sap of trees and regarded beaver's diet of tender green shoots and leaves with distaste.

"Wait awhile," said beaver. "I am almost finished with my lodge, and I need you to stand guard in case bear returns."

But porcupine's belly began rumbling as he thought of the tasty food that awaited him in his own home.

"I am leaving," he announced firmly. "You can come with me to my house if you like, but I cannot stay here any longer."

With those words he waddled off into the woods, and his friend beaver had no choice but to follow. When the pair reached the tree that was porcupine's home, the bristly animal scurried up the tree to find his meal. Beaver paced uneasily near the base of the tree, for he was not built for climbing the smooth tree trunk. He was right to be nervous. Bear had followed the two to porcupine's house and now emerged from the woods, sniffing hungrily.

"Friend porcupine!" shouted beaver. "What shall I do? The bear is coming closer!"

Then porcupine slid quickly down to the base of the tree and said, "Quick, friend. Climb on my back and I will carry you up the tree to my house."

So with beaver clinging desperately to porcupine's back, the pair climbed to safety, out of bear's reach.

Unfortunately for beaver, his soft body encountered quite a few of porcupine's sharp quills in the climb, and he now sat gingerly on a tree limb, howling and complaining in pain. Grudgingly, porcupine began to pull the barbs out of beaver's stomach and backside, while his friend continued to cry and carry on.

"Ungrateful beaver," grunted porcupine, a quill firmly clenched between his teeth. "Do you not realize that I saved your life once more?"

Without thanking his friend or even acknowledging his kind deed, beaver continued to whine and complain.

"I want to go home now, porcupine," he said. "Carry me down the tree, for I cannot climb down by myself."

By now porcupine was irritated by the ungrateful beaver, and thought he would teach him a lesson. He nonchalantly climbed a little higher in the tree and continued searching for his dinner, ignoring beaver.

After a time beaver realized porcupine was not going to help him, and that he would have to find a way down to the ground by himself. He carefully backed off the limb he was sitting on, pointing his broad tail downward. Then clutching the smooth tree trunk desperately with his sharp claws, he began sliding down to the ground. Faster and faster he slid until he landed on his back at the base of the tree with a loud thump, which knocked the wind out of him. Grumpily, he got to his feet and peered up the tree. Where the bark had once been smooth, it now had deep grooves cut into it from his claws. Because of beaver's journey down the tree, all bark now appears grooved in this manner.

The two animals, each sulking in his own self-righteousness, refused to see each other for quite some time. But because they were truly good friends, they missed one another's company.

One day beaver went to porcupine's house to make amends. "Friend porcupine," he called up the tree, "would you like to explore the island in the middle of the lake with me?" Porcupine agreed that he would, so the two companions traveled down to the lake shore.

"How will we get out to the island?" asked porcupine of his friend. "My body is not built for swimming."

"Oh, climb onto my back, and I will take you," replied beaver. "But please be careful where you put your quills!"

So porcupine clambered gingerly aboard beaver's back and they began swimming out to the island. Halfway out to the island, a big wave came up and doused the pair. Beaver cheerfully plunged through the wave, but porcupine, sputtering and choking, began scrambling for a better hold on his friend's back. In doing so, he accidently loosened a number of quills, piercing beaver's hide painfully.

"Ouch!" screamed beaver. "I told you to be careful!"

"I can't help it!" replied porcupine. "If you'd watch where you were swimming, I wouldn't have to hold on so tightly!"

So the banter continued back and forth until the pair reached the safety of the shore. Miffed at one another, the two friends separated, each exploring the island on his own.

When it was getting dark, beaver decided it was time to swim back to his lodge. He walked down to the water's edge and peered up and down the shore. He could see porcupine in the distance, coming toward him. Already he could hear his friend's voice, whining about the cold, wet trip home that lay ahead of him. Beaver, his hide still stinging from the sharp quills he received on the journey out, decided to teach porcupine a lesson. He plunged into the water alone, swimming strongly back to the other shore. He ignored his friend's cries for help.

"Let him find a way back home on his own," said beaver to himself.

The little porcupine wandered all around the island, looking for a way to get off. He climbed up one tree after the other, crying piteously. At last his mournful pleas carried across the lake to wolf, who took pity on the poor creature. Wolf called on the north winds to blow across the lake so that the water would freeze. In this way, porcupine was able to scramble across the ice to safety.

After that, beaver and porcupine, once such close friends, would have nothing to do with one another. And that is why people to this day fall in and out of friendships, because of the example of these two little animals so long ago.

The World of the Spirits

Myths are
metaphorical of the
spiritual potentiality in
the human being, and
the same powers that
animate our life animate
the life of the world.

—Joseph Campbell,
The Power of Myth

Return from the Spirit Land

The chief's son and his gentle and loving wife had only been married a short time when she died. So great was his pain at losing his precious wife that life no longer held meaning for him.

"Perhaps I should go to the spirit world myself," he thought.

He waited until his wife had been buried, then he put on his leggings and other fine clothes and started off. He walked all day and all night. At the edge of dawn, he came upon a very large valley. Voices without form seemed to echo in and out of the nearby forest.

At last the youth saw light through the trees and came to a wide, flat stone lying at the edge of the lake.

"You walk on death's road," whispered the voices.

"Then I travel as I wish," replied the young man, looking across the lake where he could see houses and people.

"Come and get me," he shouted.

But the people did not seem to hear him. He grew weak from calling, and finally he whispered to himself, "Why is it that they do not hear me?"

Immediately, someone on the opposite side of the lake said, "Somebody is shouting. A person has come from dream land. Let us go and bring him over."

Story collected from the mother of Katishan, chief of the Kasqague'di. Recorded in Wrangell, Alaska. She is not identified by name in source notes. Story adapted for this collection.

Soon the young man landed on the opposite shore, and there he saw his wife. He placed his hands gently on her tear-stained face and tipped her face to his.

"We are together again," he whispered softly.

The ghost people asked him to sit down in their house and eat with them. "Don't eat," his wife warned. "If you do you can never return to the other world." Although he was very hungry, he put the food aside.

"Let us go right away," his wife urged.

They crawled into a ghost's canoe and silently paddled to the flat rock where he had first called to the ghost people. The rock is called Ghost Rock, for it is at the end of life's trail. They started down the rock. At length they descended it, and by the second night they reached the youth's house.

The young man asked his wife to remain outside while he explained to his family, "I have brought my wife back."

"Bring her in, for she is always welcome," replied his father. While the son went to get his wife, the father placed a fur robe where they were to sit. When the door opened, the family saw only the young man. But then, as he moved closer to them, they thought they saw a deep shadow following him.

The young man asked his wife to sit, and he put a martenskin robe around the shadow as if there were a person sitting there. As she ate, they only saw the arms of the martenskin robe and the spoon moving up and down.

After a time the people got used to the strange sight. Wherever the man went, the shadow followed. During the day the woman was very quiet, but all night long the two could be heard talking. At that time her voice could be heard very plainly.

The young man's father joked with his daughter-in-law. "You'd better get up now, after keeping people awake all night with your chattering." He heard the shadow's deep laugh and recognized it as the voice of the dead woman.

Another young man in the village had been very much in love with the woman, although she did not care for him. He was jealous that her husband had brought her back.

One night she told her husband that she was going to leave her shadow self and return to her true form and remain so permanently. The rejected suitor was lurking outside their sleeping quarters and heard everything she said.

He lifted the curtain surrounding them. The moment he did so, the people heard a rattle of bones. That instant the husband died, and the ghosts returned to the land of the dead.

The Woman Who Married the Dead Man

Once there was a young woman, the daughter of a chief, who was known among the Coho people as one pure of mind and spirit. One day, when she was out walking, she tripped over something round and white with dark, gaping holes in the center. When she looked more closely she found that it was a skull.

"How horrible," she shuddered. "I pray that the spirit of the dead one leaves me in peace." She kicked the skull to one side and ran into the house, trembling.

That night the girl dreamed that two boys came to her. They were handsome, with dark, piercing eyes and shining black hair. The young men explained, "We are the sons of a nearby chief. We have lost our way after a hunting accident. May we rest awhile before we resume our travels?" In reality, they came from the spirit world. The skull she had kicked aside had once belonged to the elder son.

He spoke now in an earnest and compelling way. "I have traveled more worlds than you shall ever know, yet I can travel no longer unless you will be my wife." In what she thought was a dream, the girl consented to his proposal and they were married at once.

The next morning the chief said, "What is wrong with my daughter? She hasn't awakened yet." A servant girl hurried to the chief's daughter. She was surprised to hear several voices behind the

Story collected from the mother of Katishan, chief of the Kasqague'di. Recorded in Wrangell, Alaska. She is not identified by name in source notes. Story adapted for this collection.

robes that divided the daughter's sleeping area from the rest of the house.

"Tell my father that I was wed during the night," said the young woman.

The servant reported what she had heard. Her mother said, "That's impossible! She doesn't even know a young man nor has she had one visit her as a suitor."

Just then the girl walked into the room with her two night visitors. How proud she was of her handsome husband! Her family, however, cringed in horror, for what appeared to her to be a fine young chief, to them was a hideous skeleton.

The parents decided to humor both their daughter and the visitors lest the visitors take her off to an untimely death. "Our food is meager, but we share all that we have," said the chief as he passed the food with a trembling hand.

"Wife, ask your father if I may take his small canoe to go hunting," asked the skeleton. She did so, and soon the servant ran down to the beach to ready it for them. He found that it was missing, however. "No matter," said the skeleton. He and his brother stood in the middle of the room. First they acted as if they entered the canoe, squatting carefully between the gunwales. Then the two continued their strange charade. For all the world, they appeared to be on the sea. They paddled the canoe, speared seals, fished for halibut, and hunted for sea lions. The girl hid her face in shame at their demented actions.

All day long the play continued. As night fell, her husband turned to her and said, "Tell the people to go down to our canoe on the beach and bring back the bounty of our hunt."

Although it seemed foolish, her father and mother walked to the beach. There they saw their canoe loaded with all kinds of fish, seals, and sea lions. The chief gave each family a seal, feeding the entire village with food from the hunt.

It seemed as if the people of the village would never know hunger again, for each day the young men provided groundhogs, mountain sheep, and harvest from the sea. As the days passed the men seemed to come to life. Their skeletal forms began to shimmer, and the faint outlines of their true human selves began to materialize. Each day the human forms became more distinct.

The villagers were most grateful to the young men for their industriousness. All of them, that is, except one. Living in the village was a jealous young woman.

"Why should the chief's daughter have two such fine young men living in her family's dwelling place, when I have none?" she asked herself.

She dressed in her finest clothes and did everything she could think of to attract the attention of the younger man. When he showed no interest in her, she grew angrier and angrier. She decided to have her revenge.

In the evening she watched where the younger man sat to eat his evening meal. The next day she marked his place with human blood. That evening he sat in his usual place. When he touched the human blood, he cried out in pain. His human form disintegrated and his skeleton dropped into a pile of bones, parched and lifeless.

The jealous woman was not content. "I am much more beautiful than the chief's daughter," she told herself. "I shall have her husband."

Although the woman tried to gain his attention, the older brother had eyes only for his wife. "I'll teach him to ignore me," thought the vengeful woman.

That evening she marked the other young man's place with human blood. When he sat with his wife that evening and touched the blood, he, too, changed into a lifeless pile of bones.

Without their great hunters, the people of the village became as poor and hungry as before. Life was hard on all the people, but none suffered more than the jealous young woman. Although her stomach gnawed from hunger, the woman feared more the pain she would suffer when she herself had to go to the spirit world. Two young men waited for her there, and revenge would be theirs.

The Image That Came to Life

A young chief who lived on the Queen Charlotte Islands married, and soon afterwards his wife fell ill. He called for the best shamans in the islands to come tend to his wife. Even though they made healing brews and chanted their incantations, she grew paler and weaker by the day.

Finally the worried chief sent his canoe to bring back the greatest of all shamans, who lived in a distant village. But alas, before the canoe could return, his wife left this world.

So great was the chief's despair, the people feared for his health. One day as he was wandering from place to place, he met a carver and asked him to create a likeness of his wife.

When the chief viewed the finished likeness he said, "This work does not honor my wife."

The chief called all the great carvers and set them to work on the likeness. But all of them failed, and the chief sunk deeper into melancholy. When the chief had dismissed the last of the great carvers, he heard a gentle rap at the door. A young man stood there with eyes downcast.

"Oh, Great Chief, I am not one of the great carvers of our village, but I have often admired your wife as she walked with you in the twilight. I can still see her delicate features and radiant eyes as she

Story collected from the mother of Katishan, chief of the Kasqague'di. Recorded in Wrangell, Alaska. She is not identified by name in source notes. Story adapted for this collection.

looked up to your face. It would be a great honor if I might try to create her likeness."

"The others have failed," said the chief. "What is one more? Try if you please."

The young carver found a beautiful piece of red cedar. Day and night he coaxed the likeness of the young woman from the wood. The flowing grain of the cedar soon wrapped around her body like her best deerskin dress. At last, the image was finished.

The chief walked into the room. Everyone could hear his sharp intake of breath. A nephew caught him as he stumbled forward.

The chief whispered, "Had I not seen her dead body with my own eyes, I would swear that she sits before me now, alive, radiant, and well. Dear carver, what may I pay you for this?"

"I did not do this for payment, Chief," answered the carver. "I hurt for you as you mourned in such sorrow for your lost one. Your happiness is payment enough."

The chief carried the sculpture home and sent four times the usual payment to the young artist. The chief dressed the image in his wife's clothes, and across her shoulders he draped her martenskin robe. As he gazed at the sculpture, he imagined that his wife had come back to him.

One day, while he sat very close to the image, he felt it move. He thought the movement was only his imagination, but he continued to watch it day by day.

The image changed imperceptibly until it truly became like a human being, yet it could not move or speak. Then, one day, the image gave forth a sound from its chest like cracking wood and the man knew that it was ill. The chief moved the image from the place where it had been sitting. There, beneath it, grew a small red cedar. This was the first of the great red cedars of Queen Charlotte Island.

Even now when people find an exceptional cedar they say, "This looks just like the baby of the great chief's wife."

People from far and near came to look at the lifelike sculpture of the chief's wife and to watch the handsome young cedar grow. Although the image of the chief's wife grew more humanlike every day and even moved a little from time to time, she never regained her voice. But this did not matter to the great chief. His wife came to him every night in his dreams and they talked long into the night until dawn chased away the gentle messenger.

The Sky Country

A man's wife was taken from him. Half crazed with grief he searched the beaches for any sign of her or her captors. The wide trail he spotted appeared to wind through the woods; however, in reality it wove its way into the sky.

As he traveled, he came upon an old campsite. There, in the cold ashes, he found a number of dentalia shells.

"They'll make a beautiful necklace," he thought as he wove them together. "They may prove to be useful."

After he had walked for several days he noticed smoke curling in the distance. Close to the source of the smoke, he came upon a woman tanning a skin. He asked if she had seen his wife. At first she wouldn't answer. In fact, she wouldn't even look up from her work and acknowledge him.

Finally he said, "I will give you this necklace if you will tell me where my wife is."

The woman looked at the necklace longingly. Finally she said, "You will find her over in the next camp." The woman put on her prize and ran down to the lake to look at her reflection in the still waters.

Just as the woman said, he found his wife in the next camp. The people who had captured her treated both of them well. In fact, the man thought, "It is almost as if I am among my brothers-in-law."

Story collected from the mother of Katishan, chief of the Kasqague'di. Recorded in Wrangell, Alaska. She is not identified by name in source notes. Story adapted for this collection.

But he was not among relatives. In reality they were being held captive by the Sky People and the Sky People were simply waiting.

The chief of the Sky People nodded and the time of waiting was over. The people kindled a great fire and the chief ordered, "Kill him!"

As the people dragged the captive man toward the fire, he cried out excitedly, "Oh, how happy I am that you are going to throw me into the fire. How I love fire. I've been cold ever since I've been here. You are so kind. At last I'll be warm. Hurry, please, it will feel wonderful."

When they heard that, the Sky People stopped dragging him toward the fire and began pulling him toward the water instead. He screamed and cried for mercy, "Please don't throw me into the water. I'll sink like a clam shell filled with mud. Anything except the water! I'm terrified of fish! I can't swim!"

He clawed and scratched, holding on to every bush as they dragged him to the lake's edge. At last with a great heave they threw him into the middle of the lake.

In a few moments he popped up and looked at them like a curious seal. The Sky People said, "Look at him. He's laughing at us."

The man chortled contentedly, "The water is just where I love to be. My uncles taught me to swim before I could walk. This is more my home than the soft earth. The water soothes me like a gentle friend."

The Sky People were ashamed that they had been tricked. They left the woman and her husband and returned to the village with downcast eyes. Although the woman and man were safe for the time being, they did not know how to get back to earth.

After walking all day they came upon the house of a strange old woman. She was really a spider and the house was her web. "I will help you get back to earth," she offered. "Crawl into my web and I will lower you down. If the web gets caught on a cloud, just jerk it backwards and forwards and it will come loose."

Before long the man and the woman were safely back on earth and the web was drawn back to the sky. The couple lived happily again as they had before the woman was taken away. Only one thing changed. Whenever they came upon a spider web, they were careful not to disturb it. Maybe the spiderwoman was helping others escape from the Sky People or maybe spiderwoman's earthly cousins were catching the choicest insects to pay tribute to the one who lives in the land beyond the clouds.

The Origin of Gonaqadē't, Monster of the Sea

Long ago, in the time of strong medicine and monsters, a high-caste man married a woman from a neighboring village. His mother-in-law and father-in-law lived with them. The mother-in-law disliked her son-in-law because he was lazy and fond of gambling.

As soon as the women finished a meal, the mother-in-law would say to the slaves, "Let the fire go out. If my worthless son-in-law cannot leave his gambling to eat with us, let him eat cold food or nothing at all."

The same thing happened every evening.

Story collected from the mother of Katishan, chief of the Kasqague'di. Recorded in Wrangell, Alaska. She is not identified by name in source notes. Story adapted for this collection.

When summer came and the salmon began to run, the people moved to a camp nearer the streams. The gambler moved with them. After he had caught a few salmon and hung them up to dry, he sharpened his stone axe and began chopping down a large tree that stood a little distance back from the stream.

Although he enjoyed gambling and was not fond of most work, the man was clever and resourceful. He had heard there was a terrible monster in a nearby lake and he had in mind to catch it. He chopped for five hours before he felled the great tree. Then he made wedges out of very hard wood and forced them into the tree in an attempt to split it lengthwise. As the tree gaped open, he forced strong wooden cross-pieces between the sections to hold them apart. He ran his line down the middle of the crevice and into the water. Then he baited his line with a salmon.

By and by he felt a tug on his line, but when he attempted to pull it in, the line broke. The man rebaited it and waited. The line moved again and he leaned into the line to bring in his catch. Suddenly, the line jerked as if it were attached to a diving whale—it would be a tough fight.

Hour after hour he pulled until at last the creature surfaced. The monster leaped toward the man but had to pass over the split of the tree to attack him. Just in time, the man kicked the crosspieces out of the tree. The wooden jaws snapped shut on the head of the monster. The monster howled in pain and dove for its home beneath the lake. The tree, too, disappeared only to reappear moments later. The monster fought for its life as it thrashed to free itself from the excruciating trap.

The struggle went on all night. As dawn breached the darkness, the monster lay still.

The man waded into the water and pulled his prize catch to shore. The monster had strong teeth and sharp claws that shone like copper. He skinned it, and after it was dry, he draped it around his body.

Slowly he entered the water. The skin directed him to dive below the surface. Soon the man found himself in the monster's house beneath the lake. He had never seen a more beautiful house.

The man returned to the shores of the lake and removed his skin, hiding it in a hole near the tree that he had cut down. He told no one about his adventure.

In late fall, after a poor fish camp, people returned to the village with their meager catch. Their provisions were soon depleted, and a famine descended upon the village. Few of the villagers would live to see the spring.

One morning the man said to his wife, "I am going away. I will return in the morning just before the ravens awake. If you hear the raven call before I return you will know that I am no longer among the living."

The man walked to his hiding place and put on the monster's skin. He swam to the house beneath the waters. From there he found a secret passage to the sea. With his sharp claws he had no trouble seizing a king salmon. Swimming back through the secret passageway, he then returned to the shore where he once again hid the skin and carried the salmon to his village. He left the fish on the beach very near his house before he retired to his bed to sleep.

The man's mother-in-law got up early and came upon the salmon. She thought that it had drifted to shore. She cooked it for all the people in the village and distributed the food, as was the custom in those days. The next evening her son-in-law repeated his dive into the sea. This time, however, he brought back two salmon. He shared his secret with his wife but told her she must not tell anyone else.

The third time the man dove, he brought back a halibut. His mother-in-law found the fish and shared it with the others, but the food did little to improve her disposition.

She grew angrier and angrier with her son-in-law. He would sleep all day, not getting up to eat until it was almost evening. Before, he arose very early in order to join his friends for gambling.

The next day she said to him, "How can you sleep all day when people are starving? If I did not go out each day to find food, the villagers would not survive the long winter." Afterwards, the man and his wife laughed about the woman's ignorant, self-righteous words.

The next evening he went out again and caught another very large halibut, which he left where his mother-in-law was sure to find it. When she found this fish, the woman thought, "I wonder what is bringing me all this luck. It must be a good spirit. I shall soon be the richest person in the world."

In the morning she said to her husband, "Husband, you shall declare that I have had a bad dream. The dream told me that it is dangerous for anyone to go out before I do in the morning." She wanted to make sure that all of the treasures from the sea were hers. Her husband did what she asked of him.

The next morning the young man got a seal and laid it down in front of their house. Later, his mother-in-law saw him and taunted him, "You lazy good-for-nothing. I think I shall never again go out to find food. The villagers will starve without me." She found the seal later that morning. She had the slaves singe the hair off and scrape it in water to make the skin white, and then they cooked it in the skin. Her husband invited everyone in the village to the feast. Many speeches told how his wife had saved the people. The woman fairly strutted about with self-importance, but she wanted even more.

In the middle of the night the old woman pretended that she was visited by spirits. She changed her voice and spoke, "I am the spirit that finds all the food. Have a mask and a special dance rattle made for me."

Her husband sent for the best carver in the town to make the things she had requested. He also gave her an apron with puffin beaks all around it.

After that the woman declared that the spirits told her where to find the food. She went about the village, shaking her rattles and speaking in her spirit voice. The whole village believed her and thought her to be a great shaman. Her son-in-law lay abed, listening. He heard her declare in her spirit voice, "Tomorrow I will bring you two seals." So the next day he made sure that he left two seals for her.

The woman treated her son-in-law worse with each passing day. She ridiculed him publicly and told people to call him "Sleeping-man."

She nagged, "If you are going to sleep all day, you shall only get the poorest of scraps to eat." And that is all she allowed him to have.

The next morning she found a sea lion which her son-in-law had caught that night. She began to believe her fantasy about the spirits and was soon ordering people about and making rules for the people to follow, as if she were indeed the greatest shaman of all time. The people believed her and obeyed.

Each time he left, the son-in-law reminded his wife, "Listen for the raven. If you hear the raven before I come home, you will know that something has happened to me."

That morning the man struggled hard to bring home a whale. He was so exhausted by the effort that he barely made it before the raven called. He slept longer than usual. His mother-in-law and the villagers laughed at him and spoke of him as one might a mongrel dog.

The mother-in-law and the villagers feasted on the whale for a long time. She filled a large number of boxes with whale oil and sold them for a good price. The villagers treated her as if she were a person of very high caste. She shared none of her food with her daughter or her son-in-law. Yet the young man said to his wife, "We will not ask for food. We will only eat what she offers us."

When the whale had been consumed, the old woman danced around the village, shaking her rattles. In her spirit voice she said, "I bring you two whales, I bring you two whales."

The son-in-law remembered that he had barely been able to bring home one whale; two might be impossible. Finally, when he felt that he had his strength back, he donned his monster suit and swam to the ocean. He caught two whales and struggled all night to bring them in. Just before dawn he pulled the first whale to the leaving place. He had just reached for the second whale when the raven cried. He dropped the tail, staggered, and breathed no more.

When his wife heard the raven's cry she reached over to pull her husband close to her. She found his bed empty. She grabbed for her clothes through her tears and ran down the steps from the high foundation of the house. The people could hear her cries as the morning light pushed away their sleep.

Her mother walked out as usual and saw the two whales lying there with the monster between them. The people appeared from their houses and they, too, saw the monster. None of them dared approach the hideous creature except the daughter.

"My husband! My husband!" she cried over and over again. The people moved even farther away because they were sure the young woman had lost her mind. Her hair flowed over the monster's chest as she sobbed against his still body. Finally, she looked up at her mother and screamed, "Where are your spirits now, Mother? You are a liar!" Then she turned to the people, "Don't you see that she is a liar and a fraud? Is this her food-finding spirit?"

She glared at her mother, the hate pouring from the deepest part of her soul. "Mother, how is it that your spirit has died? Spirits don't die, do they? If you are such a powerful shaman why don't you bring it back to life? But you can't, can you, Mother? I'll show you why."

Speaking again to the villagers, the young woman said, "Some of you who are very clean—come help me."

They moved closer and were shocked by what they saw. To them it appeared that her husband had been swallowed by the monster. Nothing except his head showed in the gaping jaws of the creature. In reality, he had died just as he was crawling out of the monster's skin.

The people helped her carry the body of her husband and the monster's skin to the edge of the lake and place them in the hollow in the tree. They saw the log, broken hammers, and wedges that showed where he had killed the monster.

The story of the young man's courage and selflessness was passed from tongue to tongue. All the people in the village heard it except one. The old woman was so ashamed that she locked her door against all visitors, and she died in the blackness of her shame several weeks later.

Every evening after his death, the young woman went to the foot of the tree where his body rested and wept. One evening, however, she saw a ripple on the water. Looking up, the woman saw the monster gliding gently through the water.

The creature swam to her and said, "Come here."

It was the voice of her husband. "Get on my back and hold tight."

She straddled his back, and together they dove into the sea to live forever in the shimmering house beneath the blue-green waters.

The people never forgot the generosity of the man-monster. They renamed him *Gonaqadē't*. Even today the people believe that those fortunate enough to see him will have good luck. People also look for his wife and their children, "Daughters of the Creek," who live at the head of every stream. They, too, carry health and good fortune to those who live by the example of the mighty *Gonaqadē't*.

The Animal Spirit Helper

Myths teach compassion for all living things . . . the sanctity of the earth itself.

—Joseph Campbell,
The Power of Myth

The Wolf Chief's Son

Famine lay heavily on a young boy's village. He watched in anguish as many people died of starvation. One day, the boy gleaned some huckleberry bushes, searching for even a small handful of berries to stem his gnawing hunger.

As he entered a clearing he came across an animal that looked very much like a dog. He put it under his blanket and carried it home to his mother.

His mother washed the little dog for him. Then the boy found some red paint that had been left by his dead uncles, and he covered the dog's face and hair until the dog was as red as an overripe salmonberry.

The next day, the boy and his dog went out to hunt. Never before had the boy seen a hunter like this one. Soon they had more grouse and other game than they could carry. When they arrived back at the village, the boy gave the game to his mother to clean and prepare. Then he went down to the stream to wash the paint off his little dog.

Each day, before they went out hunting, the boy painted the dog's legs and head with the red paint. The animal was so quick, that without the paint the boy was certain that he would not be able to track his friend. Each day, after the hunt, the boy was sure to give the best part of the game to his dog.

Story collected from an elder of the Box-house people, Dekinā′k, in Sitka, Alaska. Story adapted for this collection.

The dog became the envy of many people. The boy and his dog were feeding many families.

One time his brother-in-law said, "I want to borrow your dog."

The boy brought the little dog from the house and painted its face and feet.

Then he instructed his brother-in-law, "When you kill the first animal, cut it open quickly and give the heart and liver to the dog."

The brother-in-law took the dog to a high ridge, and there they came upon a flock of sheep. The man stood in awe as the dog ran among them, killing one after another. The man cut open the first sheep, but instead of the choicest parts, he took out the entrails and threw them in the dog's face.

"Dogs always eat the guts of animals, not the good parts," said the man.

The dog stared hard at the man then turned and ran into the high mountains. The boy watched as the brother-in-law returned from the mountains, but no dog followed.

"Where is my dog?" the boy demanded.

"The stupid cur disappeared at the start of the hunt. I had to kill all these by myself," answered the brother-in-law.

The boy knew this could not be true.

He went to his sister and requested, "Please, sister, find out what really happened to my dog."

The boy's sister felt sorry for her little brother and forced her husband to tell her the truth. Her husband showed the boy where he had last seen the dog.

At first light the boy left to find his dog. After several hours he found a red paw print. He followed the trail for a long distance until he came to a lake with a town on the other side.

An old woman appeared to him out of the mists of the lake. She asked the boy, "Grandchild, why are you here?"

"I have lost my dog, and I will search until I find it!" the boy replied.

The woman retorted, "A dog indeed, my grandson! The animal you seek is not a dog! It is the son of the Wolf Chief. He lives with his people on the other side of the lake. You can hear the people talking, if you listen carefully."

"How can I get across the lake?" asked the boy.

"My little canoe is just below here," she answered. "Take it down to the water's edge, but before you get into it, shake it and it will grow larger. Stretch yourself out on the bottom, but do not paddle. Instead, you must wish for the boat to take you to the distant shore."

The boy did as he was directed. Soon he landed very near the village. When he got out of the canoe it became so small that he could put it in his quiver, which he did.

Then he approached a group of boys and asked directions to the chief's house. They pointed to a house at the far end of the village where an evening fire burned.

To his delight, he saw the little wolf playing very near his father, the great Wolf Chief.

The little wolf knew him at once.

The Wolf Chief spoke, "You are welcome and safe here. I let my son live among you because your uncles and your friends were starving. I am pleased that you loved my son enough to travel in unknown lands to find him."

By and by he continued, "I cannot allow my son to return with you, but I will give you something else that will help you." He directed his wife, "Give the boy the fish-hawk's quill that hangs on the wall." Next he instructed the boy how to use the quill. "Whenever you meet a bear, hold the quill straight toward the animal and it will protect you."

After that he took out a blanket and said, "This blanket has strong medicine. One side is for sickness. If you put this blanket on a sick person you will make him well. If anyone hates you, put the other side on him and it will end his life. Use the blanket wisely. Fame and fortune will be your companions."

As he reflected on the power of this gift, the boy began the long journey home.

The boy thought he had only been gone for two nights, but in reality he had been away for two years. When he came within sight of his town, he met a bear. He held the quill before him as he had been instructed. The quill leaped out of his hand and pierced the heart of the bear. He removed the quill and continued his journey home.

Still closer to town, the boy came upon a flock of mountain sheep. The quill flew at the sheep with deadly accuracy. Soon all of the sheep were dead. The boy once again removed the quill from the heart of the last sheep. He took some of the meat with him and covered the rest.

The boy walked into his village and was puzzled by the sound of his own footsteps, echoing among the silent houses.

"Where have my people gone?" he thought.

As he turned the corner near his family's home, he found the lifeless bodies of his family and friends, who had died during the famine. The boy sat and wept.

Suddenly, he remembered the medicine blanket. As he laid the blanket upon the bodies of his loved ones, each individual in turn came back to life. They had been dead for such a long time that their eyes remained deep set, and it took a long time for them to feel well again.

With his quill, the young man became a greater hunter than even his little wolf brother. He kept the secret of the quill to himself. Soon people from many islands were trading with him for meat.

The boy used his blanket for both mischief and good. Sometimes he would go into a town and make well people sick with a throw of his blanket. Then for a fee he would restore the sick ones to their former good health. Other times he would use the medicine blanket to cure those who were hopelessly ill.

The young man went everywhere, healing the sick for a fee. Soon he was both the richest and the most famous man in the land.

As for the wolves, when the little wolf returned with the red paint on his paws and face, the other wolves were jealous and wanted to be painted too. The Wolf Chief, not wanting dissension among his people, declared that from this day forth all wolves would have red on their feet and around their mouths.

And so, even today, when you see a wolf, it will be marked like the Wolf Chief's son.

The Story of the Eagle Crest of the Nexa'di

There was once a poor Nexa'di man who did not know how to provide for himself or his family. He would fish from his small canoe, but the best he could manage were some small bullheads and flounder. This meager fare left his mother and brothers hungrier than ever. One day he paddled off in his canoe to try to catch some

---

Story collected from Katishan, chief of the Kasqague'di. Recorded in Wrangell, Alaska. Story adapted for this collection.

salmon. He fished all day without success. Toward evening, with hunger pains clawing his belly like a she bear, he headed his canoe toward the nearby shore. So weak was he that he trembled as he pulled the canoe onto the beach. As he did so, he heard a voice saying, "I have come for you."

The man was terribly frightened and threw himself down upon the beach and covered himself with his ragged blanket of groundhog skins. He peeked anxiously out of a hole in the blanket as the voice came closer.

"I have seen you now!" cried the voice. Powerful talons snatched the blanket away from the trembling man.

Standing before him was an eagle. The man stared as the image of the eagle shimmered and gradually assumed a human form.

Once more the eagle spoke, "My grandfather has sent me for you. You will follow me."

The man was afraid not to obey. The eagle led the way into the woods. The pair walked along the trail until they came to a set of steps which led them to a house situated just below the clouds. The eagle motioned for the man to follow him into this house. Inside everything was just like the houses of human beings, with mats strewn on the floor. The eagle guide and his people treated the man kindly, serving him enough fish and game to satisfy his gnawing hunger at last. Contented, the man asked if he might stay with the eagle people forever. Among his own kind the man was poor and low caste, but among the eagle people he was treated well.

After a time the man married one of the eagle women. For a wedding gift her brothers gave the man a beautiful coat of eagle feathers. As they draped the robe around his shoulders, the oldest brother said,

"We name this coat Camping-under-water-for-two-days (*Dex-hin-ta-de-uxe*), for a great eagle hunter may attach itself to a seal and be dragged beneath the sea for two days without the eagle losing his life. May you be as mighty as the most powerful of our forefathers."

Unknown to the man, the coat had transformed him into an eagle, and as his brother-in-laws had foretold, he became a great fisherman. All the time he thought he was spearing the fish, he was really catching them in his deadly talons.

Once, after he had snatched a particularly large fish from the water, he spied his mother and brothers struggling to catch some salmon. Swooping low over their canoe, he dropped the fish where they could find it.

Later that night the eagle man appeared to his mother in a dream.

He told her, "I am one of the eagle people now. I have married an eagle woman and cannot come among you any more. Camp with my brothers at the place where I tell you."

The next day, when his mother and brothers paddled to the spot where he had instructed them to be, the eagle flew over them, dropping a load of fish. Time after time he returned to them with his catch until they had plenty of fish to preserve and share with the whole village for months ahead.

Then the eagle flew up into a nearby tree and called, "It is I." He called down his former name and the eagle man's family marveled at his transformation.

That winter was particularly long and harsh, but thanks to the eagle, the Nexa'di people had plenty of fish to satisfy their hunger through the cold months. The Nexa'di people wished to remember the kindness of the eagle people. Thus they adopted the eagle as their crest.

On long winter's nights the old ones share this story with their grandchildren so the children will never forget. A grandfather will say, "Grandson, the eagle you see in the high cedars is a descendant of the man who used to walk among our clan. He became an eagle, mighty and strong, to save the Nexa'di people from starvation. You must live your lives so that you are worthy of the eagle crest."

The Man Who Was Abandoned

In a village, the last of the food had been eaten and the people ached with hunger. Day after day the hunters and the fishermen returned empty handed.

Living among the people was a lazy youth who did not bother to help search for food. He preferred to sleep all day.

"If my uncle, the great hunter, cannot find game, then certainly I could not. Besides, it is so cozy among these skins," said the lazy one.

Story collected from an elder of the Box-house people, Dekinā′k, in Sitka, Alaska. Story adapted for this collection.

And once again, although the sun was high in the sky, he covered his head and resumed his sleep.

His uncle said, "We must move our camp and look for food elsewhere." The uncle's wife looked down at her sleeping nephew and asked, "Shall I try to awaken him so he can go with us?" She had always felt kindly toward her nephew, for although he was the laziest young man in the world, she thought him good of heart.

"No. Leave him to the wild animals," retorted the uncle. "Let them feast, since we cannot."

His wife packed the camp and prepared to leave. She knew most certainly that her nephew would die.

"Perhaps I can give him one more day of life," she thought. She found one last piece of dried fish and laid it beside his bed before she left the camp.

His people had been gone for half a day when the youth awoke, his stomach burning with hunger. He heard strange noises. Was it his imagination or were the ghost people calling him to the world beyond? He covered his head so that he couldn't hear, but the voice grew louder and more distinct.

"I have come to help you," the voice croaked.

He peeked out from the covers, and there before him was a bluish-green frog with very large teeth.

"Put me in the ocean. It is much too far for me to walk," demanded the frog. Without thinking about the odd request, the youth carried the frog to the ocean shore, placing the frog gingerly in the frigid water. As the frog disappeared beneath the distant waves, the youth turned and walked back to the village. When he got there, he began to forage for scraps of food left by the villagers. He made a soup from a small piece of dried fish overlooked by his relatives during their hurried packing. Even if he had learned how to hunt or fish, he was much too lazy to go beyond the fringes of the village. As the day wore on, he absentmindedly looked to the ocean once and a while and thought about the strange frog. "It's too far to walk right now," he yawned. "Perhaps a little nap first. Then I'll see what the frog means about helping me."

Night fell and the youth slept. At dawn he awoke to the raucous cry of the raven on the beach below. As he approached the beach he saw the largest halibut he had ever seen floating toward the shore. He used the last of his strength to pull it ashore. As he turned the halibut over, he saw the frog, with its teeth deeply embedded in the heart of the halibut.

The young man cut out the choicest parts of the fish and fed them to his frog helper. Then he cut up the rest of the halibut to be preserved later.

Early the next morning, before daylight broke over the horizon, the lazy youth carried his helper down to the beach and carefully placed the frog in the water. Then he went back to the empty village to wait.

Toward dawn, he heard the raven call, and once again he ran down to the beach. There before him were five seals, floating one after the other. Attached to the heart of the fifth seal was the frog helper. The young man gently removed his friend and put him in a place of honor.

The youth looked up from his labors to the tops of the mountains where the treeline stopped. There he saw several mountain sheep grazing together. The young man placed the frog inside his shirt, and he climbed for several hours to reach the flock. When he got to the place where they were grazing, he put his helper down. The frog hopped among the herd of sheep and all of them fell dead.

Although the youth had enough food to feed several villages, his uncles, in a distant village, faced what seemed to be certain starvation. The hunters had fared no better in the new camp than they had in the old one. As if hunger were not enough of a concern, the aunt worried that her nephew had not had a proper burial. At her urging the uncle sent three slaves to burn his body in the Tlingit way.

As the slaves approached the village, they grew more and more apprehensive. Would the spirit of the dead youth play some mischief upon them? But to their surprise, the slaves found the youth thriving as never before. He invited them into his house and prepared for them a great feast.

"To repay me, I ask two things of you," said the youth. "First, take nothing from my house to yours. Second, tell my uncles that you found me dead and that my body has been cremated."

One of the slaves thought, "He has so much food. I must take one small piece of seal fat to my little boy. He will never miss it."

When they returned to the village, they found that two more people had died from the famine.

That night, the slave's young son began to cry, "Little fat, little fat." The slave fed his child, who screamed, "More fat, more fat!"

When his relatives saw the fat dripping from the corners of the child's mouth, they called the chief.

The slave, fearing the chief's anger, confessed, "Your nephew lives! He has enough food in his house to feed 10 villages."

The people journeyed back to their village. The chief's nephew fed all of the villagers gladly, except for his uncle, who had demanded that he be left to die alone.

"Leave him to die as he left me," chided the young man, his pride wounded to the quick.

The people wondered, "How can this young man be so successful? Even though his house is filled with food, he continues his lazy ways. He lies about in his sleeping robes for half of the day. He rarely leaves the cooking fire except to make water."

The people didn't see him take the frog out of the special box each evening to hunt for him. He always made sure that the frog got the choicest pieces of meat before he slipped his helper back into the box.

Soon the lazy youth was rich beyond his imagination. People journeyed from afar to trade slaves, blankets, knives, and other goods for food.

One day the young man sent his frog helper out and it came back with a whale. Gleefully, the lazy youth fantasized about all the riches this latest and biggest harvest would bring. He was so excited that he forgot to detach his friend from the heart of the whale.

Three days later the youth remembered his helper. Although he looked for miles up and down the beach, he could not find the frog. Without his helper, he was nothing. It wasn't long before his great stores of food were gone.

The lazy youth began trading his great stores of riches for dried berries and salmon. Soon he was left with nothing but his ragged sleeping robe. Although he was now as poor as before, the man continued his lazy ways. He remained curled up in his filthy robe until the sun was high in the sky each day.

One day, however, hunger forced the young man from his sleep earlier than usual. He wandered far down the coast, hoping to find his small helper somewhere along the beach.

As the people watched his gaunt figure grow smaller and smaller in the distance, they said, "That is the last we will ever see of that lazy young man."

They were right, for he never returned from his futile walk.

Even today Tlingit people warn their children, "Watch out, or you will be abandoned like the lazy man!"

Little Felon

Once a man had an infection in his finger that pulsed with pain day and night. Pain is a poor sleeping companion. After three nights with little sleep, the man told a friend that he would do anything to relieve the discomfort.

The friend suggested, "First, make your knife clean by heating it over the fire. Give me the knife and hold your finger under the smokehole of the house. I will climb onto the roof and reach down through the smokehole with the sharp point. Then I will cut open the infected area and let it drain, and you will be cured."

The man did as his friend suggested. As the finger drained the man noticed something that looked like two tiny eyes. He wrapped them up in a cloth and laid them by his sleeping place.

Late in the evening he looked at the cloth, and there, sitting where the eyes had been, was a tiny man about one inch tall. The man took very good care of the little man, and soon he became large enough to run about. The man named him Little Felon.

Little Felon was as industrious as he was talented. He carved, made canoes, and painted. He was also an excellent hunter and a very fast runner. Whenever Little Felon labored, the man could not help but join him. Together they could do the work of four men.

(*Felon* means an infection at the end of the finger near or around the nail or bone.)

Story collected from an elder of the Box-house people, Dekinā'k, in Sitka, Alaska. Story adapted for this collection.

One day the man noticed a very pretty girl walking by the stream. He asked others about her and found that she lived with her grandmother. Although many fine young men went to court her, none of them returned. The grandmother forced all of the girl's suitors to guess the kind of animal skin she was wearing. If they were incorrect, she put them to death.

The young man told Little Felon about the girl. Little Felon said, "I know what kind of a skin it is. One day the grandmother caught a louse and fed it until it grew large. When it was just the right size she killed it and skinned it. Now she wears it as a hideous cloak. If you go to visit her, be very careful. The old woman knows about medicines and magic. When you go toward her, go with the wind. Never approach her when a south wind is blowing. Some people have gone directly to her and they were put to death. She cooks their bodies in a large square dish."

The youth approached the old woman's camp, but a strong south wind was blowing. He waited a long time. At last, the wind shifted to the north, and he moved toward the camp.

As he approached, the old woman said, "Oh! My grandson, please come and eat with us."

The young man ate heartily. As he was finishing, the old woman asked, "What kind of skin is this?"

He answered, "Why, the skin of a large louse, Grandmother."

"What a wise young man you are," replied the old woman. "I've been looking for one such as you to marry my granddaughter. But first, do you see that dark cove over there? A very large devilfish lives there. I want you to kill it."

The youth went home and told Little Felon what she had said.

"Ahh, she plans to rid herself of you in that way. We will out-smart her," said Little Felon. Little Felon made a special hook and caught the devilfish. He gave the devilfish to the young man and said, "You must be careful and carry it just as I show you or harm may come to you."

Carrying the devilfish exactly as he had been shown, the youth arrived at the old woman's house. "Is this the devilfish you were talking about?" asked the youth. When the young man threw it down he saw it twist and turn. In moments the devilfish grew into a monster that filled the entire house.

"Take that disgusting thing out of here," commanded the old woman. The moment he touched it, it became small again, and he tossed it outside.

The old woman muttered to herself. At last she turned to the youth. "Do you see that cliff that goes down to the water? A monster rat lives there. If you kill it, you shall have my granddaughter."

Little Felon and the boy readied their arrows and crawled silently to the hole of the monster. They shot arrow after arrow, and at last, they mortally wounded the rat. With one last surge of life, the monster rat charged at them. The boy feinted and moved out of the rat's reach. The rat plunged into the ocean, where he thrashed about helplessly. After a time the rat was still. The boy pulled the rat from the water and carried it to the house of the old woman.

"Is this the rat you wished for me to kill?" asked the boy. As he threw it down it filled the house.

"Remove it at once," she said. Her face twisted and her lip twitched. She paced back and forth. Forcing a thin smile, she sneered,

"Grandson, way out in the depths of the ocean is a sculpin. You must get it for me if you are to have my granddaughter."

Little Felon knew which sculpin the old hag required. They paddled their canoe to a dangerous part of the ocean where the currents had carried many good men to their untimely deaths. Little Felon dove beneath the waves and returned in a few moments with a small sculpin. He threw the catch into the bottom of the canoe and they paddled home.

When they arrived on shore, the youth carried the sculpin to the old woman's house. No sooner had he laid it on the floor than it grew into a monster with great deadly spines filling every corner of the house.

"Get it out of here," she shrieked.

Now the old woman didn't know what to do. "What kind of a boy is this," she thought. "He has killed all the things that were dear to me. I will give him one last task. Surely he will fail with this one."

She spoke to the boy. "Go far out to sea beyond the place where you got that sculpin. I dropped my bracelet overboard there. Go and get it."

"Good riddance," she thought to herself. "The sea is so deep there that any human that tries to dive into her depths will be crushed like a pine cone beneath a giant's foot." She chuckled at the thought.

Before they left to find the bracelet, Little Felon and the youth dug a quantity of clams and placed them in their canoe. When they reached the appointed place, Little Felon opened the clam shells and threw the meat into the water. Before long, all kinds of fish were coming to feed. A dogfish came by and Little Felon said, "Friend fish, if

you will go to the depths of the sea and retrieve a lost bracelet, I will give you the rest of these choice clams."

Since the dogfish loved nothing better than clams, he retrieved the bracelet in no time at all.

When the old woman saw her bracelet she trembled, thinking, "Perhaps the boy is not human after all, but is a spirit sent to punish me for my treachery." She addressed the boy: "Marry her, my grandson. I am done with you."

After the wedding celebration, the young man asked Little Felon what he owed him for his help.

"You don't owe me anything. It was you that freed me from my prison," the small one answered. With that Little Felon ran to the ocean and resumed his natural form. He is the eulachon, a slender fish that swims close to the beach.

As for the young man and his bride, they didn't live happily ever after, but that is another story.

Stories That Teach the Values of the Culture

The images of myth
are reflections of the
spiritual potentials of
every one of us.
Through contemplating
these, we evoke their
powers in our own lives.

—Joseph Campbell,
The Power of Myth

The Boy Who Shot the Star

Back in the time of magic and mystery, when bears could talk and the moon danced in the sky, two boys were the best of friends. The two would work for many hours making many arrows so they could play The Great Hunter game. The boys would imitate the great hunts of the men of their village. Bushes became bears, logs were killer whales, exposed tree roots became blacktail deer. Each day they would hunt until their arrows were exhausted.

Story collected from the mother of Katishan, chief of the Kasqague'di. Recorded in Wrangell, Alaska. She is not identified by name in source notes. Story adapted for this collection.

One day the boys had a contest to see who could make the most arrows. The moon had started to rise when the younger boy conceded, "I yield to you, my friend. My fingers are so sore; I can do no more. You are the great chief of the arrow makers."

"I am indeed," said the older one good-naturedly. "I'll race you to the top of the hill. Let's stand on top and see who can shoot an arrow the farthest."

The boys sprinted up the hill until at last they reached the smooth, grassy hilltop that often served as their playground. The older boy reached the top first and lay gasping for breath in the moonlight.

As he looked at the dark shadows of the moon's surface he said, "Look at the face on the moon. How unbelievably ugly she is. She looks like my grandmother's labret."

"Don't," whispered the younger boy. "You must not speak of the moon that way. She'll be angry." A shiver passed through the older boy as he heard his friend speak, for he knew that the young boy spoke the truth.

The night air, which earlier had felt soft and inviting, now felt threatening. As the boys made ready to return to the safety of their houses, a darkness, black and sinister, enveloped them. It was as if a giant hand had snatched the moon and stars from the sky, leaving behind inky blackness. The howling sound that followed would have made even their great chief himself shiver with fear. A rainbow shot out of the black void and curled round and round the boys.

The younger boy huddled on the ground until the specter vanished. When he dared to look up he saw that the moon and stars were back in the sky, but where was his friend? Had the moon's messenger carried him off?

At first the young boy covered his head and cried piteously for his lost friend. Then he began to get angry. He shouted at the moon, "How dare you take the great chief of the arrow makers from this earth! I'll teach you and your friends a lesson. I'll pierce the hearts of your friends, the stars, until you are alone in the sky as I am on earth."

With that the boy took aim at the star next to the moon. His arrow flew toward the glowing heart of the moon's brightest companion. As he watched, the star darkened. He shot arrow after arrow into the sky and none returned to the earth.

After a time the boy noticed that something was hanging down very near to him. He shot an arrow at it, and the arrow stuck to the bottom of the object. Arrow after arrow he let fly until the arrows formed a chain that seemed to reach to him.

His anger and his arrows spent, the young boy laid upon the grassy hill and cried once more for his lost friend. Soon he was asleep.

When he awoke he looked heavenward. Much to his surprise, his chain of arrows had disappeared, and in its place was a ladder.

The ladder beckoned, "Little boy, climb me and I shall show you worlds unimagined. Come, little boy, come. You must bring something of your world to the sky world. Come, little boy, quickly! Soon it will be light."

What could the young boy bring from this world? He didn't have time to get dried fish and berries. Instead, he gathered small branches from various nearby bushes. He stuck the twigs into his hair so that his hands would be free to climb.

As dawn crept from her drowsy sleep, the boy began his ascent. He climbed the ladder all day and camped upon it at nightfall. As he resumed his journey the next morning, his head felt very heavy. He seized the salmonberry bush that he had stuck in his hair and found it loaded with berries. He ate the berries and felt much strengthened. After that he resumed his climb. About noon he again felt hungry, and his head felt heavy. The boy pulled a bush out of the other side of his head and found it loaded, too—with blue huckleberries this time.

The young boy made camp upon the ladder. When he awoke in the morning, he continued climbing. At noon, his head began to feel heavy again. He reached to the back of his head and found red huckleberries growing there. "Ahh, food for another day," he thought.

Late in the day the boy reached the top of the ladder. He staggered with exhaustion and was asleep before he could gather soft moss for his bed.

While he slept, he dreamed that a fair young woman called to him, "Get up. I come for you." So real was the image that he awoke with a start. He looked around but no one was there. He rolled over and pretended to sleep, but looked out through his eyelashes. By and by a very small but handsome girl reached out to him. Her clothes were made of soft deerskin, and her leggings were adorned with porcupine quills.

The girl whispered, "I have come for you. My grandmother has sent me to bring you to her house." The boy rose up and followed her to a little house near a great lake. An old woman was waiting at the door.

The old woman said, "Why do you enter the land above, my grandson?"

"Good grandmother," answered the young boy, "my companion was taken from our world and I wish to find him. I fear for his life."

"Oh!" answered the old woman. "He is only a short distance away. I hear him crying every day. He is being held captive by the moon. But you must be strong if you are to rescue him. I will give you food." Then the old woman put her hand to her mouth and a salmon appeared. When she reached to her mouth again, meat and berries poured forth.

After the young boy had eaten his fill she gave him four objects: a spruce cone, a rose bush, a piece of devil's club, and a small piece of whetstone.

"You may find these helpful," said the old woman. "The moon is difficult to defeat."

The boy thanked the old woman and left to find his friend. As he got closer to the moon's house he heard his companion's cries. The older boy had been placed on a high platform near the smokehole. The younger boy climbed on the roof and pulled his friend out through the smokehole. Putting the spruce cone down where his friend had been, the boy told it to imitate the older boy's cries.

The boys climbed down from the roof and ran toward the ladder. The spruce cone cried so hard that it became dislodged from the platform and fell right in the middle of the moon's house.

"My captive has escaped," cried the moon. The moon started in pursuit of the two boys.

The boys turned to see the moon closing the gap between them. In desperation, the younger boy threw the devil's club behind him. Instantly, a thick forest of devil's club grew up. It slowed the moon for a moment, but she used her magic to cut through it.

When the moon again approached, the boy threw down the rose bush, and such a thicket of roses grew that the moon was again delayed. But the moon was powerful and she broke through the thicket.

Now the two boys were nearly in her reach. The younger boy threw down the whetstone, their last talisman. The stone became a high cliff. Again and again the moon climbed the cliff, only to be rolled back each time.

At last the boys reached the place where the ladder had been, but they were disappointed to find it destroyed.

"It's been dashed to bits," cried the younger boy. "Must we live in the sky world forever?"

Then the old woman appeared and said, "I will help you return to your world. First, you must lie down and think only of your favorite place on top of the hill. Don't think of anything else except that playground."

The boys concentrated hard, but after a time the older one thought of the old woman's house, and immediately the two boys found themselves back there.

The old woman said, "Try again. This time, think only of your beloved playground."

Again the boys focused their thoughts on the grassy hilltop, and when they awoke they were lying on their playground at the foot of the broken ladder. They heard the drum calling the villagers to a death feast. They watched the people walking somberly, their faces blackened and their eyes reddened with tears.

"I wonder who died," thought the older boy.

"Look there, at our mothers. They mourn for us," exclaimed his friend.

The older boy saw his younger brother walk by, and he called to him, "Brother, come here. It is I."

The little boy was afraid that the apparition would take him to the spirit world so he ran to the safety of his house.

"Mother," said the little brother, "my brother calls to me outside our house."

"You foolish child," answered the mother, "your brother is dead."

The boy continued to call to his little brother. "Please, little brother, take this shirt to my mother so that she'll know that I am indeed alive."

Finally the little boy bravely approached his brother and saw that he was not from the land of the dead.

"They are alive! They are alive!" he called. The villagers rejoiced at the safe return of the two young companions.

The older boy learned his lesson. He never again said unkind things about the moon. "You never know when she might find a way over that cliff," he thought.

The Salmon Chief

The seas, angry and vengeful, pulled a young man's small canoe deep into the valley of her waves. He turned his canoe to shore to escape the sea's hungry fingers. Although the young man was safe for the moment, he dragged his canoe up onto the beach with a heavy heart.

Seven days he had gone out to sea and seven days he had come home empty handed. Weary and despondent, he turned toward his

Story collected from the mother of Katishan, chief of the Kasqague'di. Recorded in Wrangell, Alaska. She is not identified by name in source notes. Story adapted for this collection.

home. As he worried about how he and his wife would survive, he glanced down at the beach, and there he saw a salmon which had been left by the tide.

"At last, a good meal for my wife and me," he thought.

As the man reached down to pick up the glistening salmon, the fish spoke to him, saying, "No, no, don't eat me! I am the chief of all the salmon. If you let me go you shall never be hungry again."

The young man had never before heard a talking fish, so, whether it was from shock or fear, he threw the salmon king back into the water of the inlet. The moment the salmon dove for the ocean depths, the sea became quiet.

"What a strange event," thought the man to himself. "I have a few hours before dark. I'll see if the fish speaks the truth." The man returned to the water. Each time he cast his salmon hook into the sea, he pulled in a fine salmon. His canoe was soon so full of fish that he feared it might founder with the weight.

The next day the seas were even more stormy than before. The man ran down to the beach to secure his canoe. Again near his boat, he found a big, fat salmon lying helplessly on the beach.

"This one is even bigger than the one before," he thought. "I suppose I will have to return it to the sea."

The salmon spoke at once, saying, "Don't let me go. Instead, you must take me home and have me for supper. But take care. You must not break any of my bones. Place the bones from my head under your pillow tonight. Sleep well. In the morning you shall be rewarded."

The man lived alone with his wife. Although they had been married for many years, they had no children. Around midnight, the man and his wife awoke to sounds like gulls crying. The sound seemed to be coming from their bed. Peering under their pillow, they found two fine-looking baby boys. The man and his wife were delighted.

The children grew up fast but were so different from one another that the people in the village wondered if they were truly brothers. One was daring and brave, with boundless energy and curiosity. The other was timid and cowardly, never venturing too far from home.

"Father," asked the brave son, "what worlds lie beyond the distant horizon, where the sun hides during the night and the moon hides by day?"

"The world is as you see it. There is nothing beyond the distant sea," replied the father, for he feared his son would leave them. When his son asked to see for himself, his father refused.

The boy begged day and night, "Please let me go, Father. I will return. I must find out what more there is to the world."

Finally, his father gave in, and the despondent parents prepared food for their son's departure. At first light the brave son paddled out to sea. His parents watched until the canoe became as small as a salmonberry seed and disappeared over the horizon.

The boy journeyed for many days until, at last, he saw a distant body of land. As he paddled closer, the beach and the forest looked very much like his homeland. He saw smoke curling from distant houses. He beached his canoe and walked toward the village. When he drew closer to the houses, he could see that this place wasn't at all like home. The village was somber, dark, and silent, in contrast to the green and inviting forest that surrounded it. Presently he came to a house where an old woman lived.

"My grandson," she exclaimed, "come and eat with me."

After he had eaten he asked, "Grandmother, why is this village so quiet and dark?"

She answered, "A monster lives beyond the ridge. It is hideous, with a human form, yet seven heads appear where there should be one. The monster demands the life of the chief's daughter, or else he will destroy the village. She willingly goes to her death to spare the people. The people now walk to deliver her to the monster."

In the distance he heard the somber drums and saw the villagers dancing a slow, mournful dance as they carried the chief's daughter up the ridge. The boy ran toward the ridge and arrived at the top just as the chief's daughter stumbled from the crowd to face her death.

He grabbed the young woman and said, "You shall not die alone." He too stepped toward the monster's den. The earth shook and a stench poured from the mouth of the cave. Seven grotesque heads appeared.

The monster laughed, "I thought I was going to have just one girl to eat, but I am also going to have a fine, plump boy."

"You will have to fight me first," the boy answered.

The monster sneered, "Do you see all those human bones, broken and parched? Many men mightier than you have tried to defeat me. Lie down and die, you miserable insect." With that the monster darted forward with one head. The boy feinted to the left, then slashed to his right, cutting off the head with his knife. Quickly the boy moved again and destroyed another head. The monster stumbled backward. One more head fell to the ground as the boy struck again with his knife.

"I am stronger now with four heads than I was with seven," roared the monster as his jaws descended on the boy's uplifted arm.

The boy moved with the grace of a porpoise and the power of a killer whale. The jaws missed their target, snapping shut on empty space. The monster howled in frustration as it became more and more disoriented and confused. Time and time again the terrible jaws missed their mark. The boy was quick. Each time the monster lurched forward the boy chopped off another head. At last the monster lay still, his lifeblood spilled upon the ridge.

"You have saved my daughter and our people," the chief proclaimed. "I will give you whatever riches you desire."

"I have only one desire, Great Chief. I wish to marry your daughter," answered the young man.

Although the boy was from a low-caste family, the chief consented immediately. Not only did he give his daughter to the young man as his bride, but he also sent many lavish gifts to the boy's family in gratitude.

The village was saved, the young woman lived, and a childless couple was rewarded with children and lavish gifts. All because a man had followed the commands of the salmon chief and a boy had dared to ask, "What worlds lie beyond the distant horizon, where the sun hides during the night and the moon hides by day?"

The Man Who Entertained the Bears

A man lived happily among his people, who were of a Raven clan. One day he returned from hunting and found that all of his family and friends had been killed. He could not bear to live without them, even though a few of his clan remained.

He thought, "If I go in search of another village, the people may think that I am a witch who destroyed my own clan. How disgraceful that would be! Perhaps I could take my own life and join those who are now journeying to the spirit world."

Story collected from the mother of Katishan, chief of the Kasqague'di. Recorded in Wrangell, Alaska. She is not identified by name in source notes. Story adapted for this collection.

He walked through the forest, trying to summon enough courage to kill himself. Finally a plan occurred to him.

"I will find the bears and let them do the work for me," he said to himself.

At the mouth of a large salmon creek he found a bear trail. He lay down across it, thinking the bears would kill him as soon as they came to fish in the stream.

By and by he heard the bushes breaking and saw many huge grizzly bears coming toward him. The man was terrified and imagined himself dying a terrible death as they tore him limb from limb. The largest bear, with powerful jaws and white-tipped fur, leaned toward him.

As the bear opened his jaws the man said in a quaking voice, "I have come to invite you to a feast." The bear's jaws clamped shut and his fur stood on end.

"I have come to invite you to a feast, but, if you are going to kill me, I am willing to die. I am alone. I have lost all my property, my children, and my wife."

The giant bear turned and whined to the bears that followed him. They lumbered back the way they had come.

The man got up and hurried toward his village. He began to make preparations for the feast. First he replaced the old sand around the fireplace with clean sand. As he collected a load of wood, he told the other people in his village about the bear feast.

"What made you do such a thing?" asked the frightened villagers.

Very early the next morning the man took off his shirt and painted himself with a red stripe across his upper arm muscles, a stripe over his heart, and another across his upper chest. Thus prepared, he stood outside the door, watching for his guests.

The brush snapped and out of the forest came the bears, led by the Great One. The villagers were so frightened they shut themselves away in their houses.

The man stood still to receive them. He invited them into his house. He gave the bear chief the place of honor, seating the others around him. First he served large trays of cranberries preserved in grease. The great bear accepted the dish and the other bears followed. The host served dish after dish: dried salmon, delicate herring eggs, venison dipped in eulachon oil. The bears ate hungrily, each carefully following the example of the Great One.

When all the food was eaten the large bear rose on his powerful hind legs and, in a strange whining voice, seemed to talk to the man for a very long time. It was almost as if he were making a speech. At last the Great One dropped to all fours and prepared to leave, but first he walked over and licked the paint from their host's arm and breast. Each bear in turn did the same thing.

"What a strange evening it has been," thought the man as the bears departed. "The Great One seems almost human."

The next day the man was fishing by the salmon stream when a small bear ambled over to him. As the man gazed upon his visitor, the image of the bear became more and more transparent, and from it emerged the shape of a man.

The bear-man spoke to the man in Tlingit, "Long ago I was a man, but I was captured and adopted by the bear clan. Now I am willingly one of them. The bear chief sent me to you. Did you understand his speech last night?"

"Although I tried hard to listen and imagine what he was saying, I fear that I could make no meaning of it," answered the man.

"The bear chief says that his heart and yours are one in their trouble and pain. Long ago the bear chief also lost his family and friends. He shares your tears as you mourn for those that are no longer of this world," said the bear-man.

"Please tell the chief that we are brothers," answered the man, deeply moved.

The Tlingit people remember this story of the man and the bear. Even today some of the old ones paint a cross on the body of the dead grizzly bear at the conclusion of their hunt. Also, when a Tlingit gives a feast, all are invited, friend and foe alike. For like the man and the bears, any mortal enemy may become a friend.

The Mountain Dweller

Two high-caste young women had entered puberty and were secluded behind a screen in their family's house, in the usual Tlingit manner. Their mother spent time instructing the sisters in the songs and legends of their clan, as well as in the manners and duties of women. In this way the girls were kept chaste and pure until the time came for them to be brides. The young women were allowed to eat only what was brought to them by their mother at mealtimes, and they were forbidden to eat anything between meals. Because their family was high-caste, the girls were expected to bring a high bride price to the family.

The girls' father was an important man in the town, and he often had people visiting him. He kept a box of seal oil to serve to his guests on these occasions. During their time of seclusion, the girls were forbidden to look upon the box or any other ceremonial articles, for fear they would bring misfortune and dishonor upon their house.

One day a large canoe landed on the beach, bringing a party of foreigners ashore. The man went down to invite the visitors to his house for a meal. The other members of his family, filled with curiousity about the newcomers, followed him. The two young women were left behind in the house.

Story collected from an elder of the Box-house people, Dekināk, in Sitka, Alaska. Story adapted for this collection.

"Sister, I long for a taste of the seal fat our father keeps in his special box," said the younger girl to her sister.

"Hush! Don't even speak of such a shameful idea!" replied the elder sister. But the seeds of desire were planted in her mind by her sister's comment, and her mouth too began to water for a taste of the delicacy.

Once again the younger girl spoke, "Sister, what harm could it do just to take a tiny taste of the fat? The ceremony won't begin for hours, and our mother will likely forget us behind this screen she will be so busy serving the others."

The older girl began to weaken as she thought of the taste and feel of the rich tallow melting in her mouth.

"We will only take a small scoop each and then come right back to our place," whined the young girl.

At last she persuaded her sister, and the pair darted out from behind the screen. They located the box in the back of the house, where their father kept many sacred objects. Giggling nervously, they pried the lid off the box and gazed hungrily at the contents within. They dipped their hands into the rich tallow and licked the delicious fat off their fingers, one by one. Unable to stop with just one taste, the girls scooped more and more of the rich contents into their mouths, until at last their fingers scraped the bottom of the box. Horrified thinking of the consequence of their foolish actions, the older sister wiped her mouth hastily with the back of her hand and replaced the lid on the box. Then she grabbed her sister's greasy hand in her own and dragged her back behind the screen where they cowered together, awaiting their family's return.

The foreign people were all seated, as was the custom, and the girl's father ordered the big box to be brought before him in order to serve the guests. When the box was opened, the man was greatly humiliated to discover it was completely empty.

Their mother, suspecting the truth, went behind the screen to question the girls. She looked at them closely.

"Did you do this?" she queried angrily.

The older girl had wiped all traces of the grease from her hands and face, but the younger girl still had smudges of oil around her mouth. She furiously tried wiping the telltale stuff away with her hair, but she was caught by her angry mother. The woman jerked her daughter's mouth open and inserted her fingers to feel for any remaining grease. In doing so she scratched the girl's palate badly, and the girl cried out in pain.

"So," cried the older woman, "you bring disgrace on your father's house."

Then she turned her wrath on her older daughter, who could not hide the guilt on her face. Grabbing the girl's face, she clawed it with her rough nails.

"You are fit to marry no man but the Mountain Dweller!" she said in disgust and left the two girls to their shame.

The Mountain Dweller, so named because he lived on the mountain, was a powerful being. Even though the girls knew no one returned from visits to his mountains, they plotted to run away to him so great was their shame. As their family slept, they slipped out from behind the screen and into the woods.

The next morning their mother went behind the screen to wake them. As she pulled back the sleeping robes, she was dismayed to find that the girls were no longer there. The people began searching for the two young women in the woods nearby. They searched for seven days, but no trace of the girls was found. The villagers returned, mourning the loss of the pair.

Meanwhile, the girls climbed higher and higher into the mountains, growing weary and famished. At length, they stopped to rest on a fallen log and were startled by a small mouse scurrying over the dead limb. The little creature was carrying a ripe huckleberry in its mouth.

"Oh, how I wish we had some of those berries to eat," said the younger sister hungrily.

The mouse paused, then crept timidly up to the girl and dropped the huckleberry into her lap. As the girl popped it eagerly into her mouth, the little mouse spoke.

"Follow me," he said, "and I will show you where to find more of the berries."

The two young women followed the mouse. True to his word, the mouse led them to a large patch of huckleberries, where the girls ate and ate until their hands and faces were stained red with the sticky juice.

"What are you doing so far from home?" asked the mouse, as he watched the pair devour the berries.

"We seek the Mountain Dweller," answered the older girl. "Our mother said we are fit to be only his brides. Can you show us where he lives?"

At the mention of the Mountain Dweller, the little mouse trembled.

"I will point you in the direction of his house," he answered, "but I will not go near it."

"Why not?" asked the younger girl, her curiosity aroused. "Is he an evil being?"

"I am not afraid of the Mountain Dweller," answered the mouse, "for he is kind and gentle and generous. In his house he keeps great stores of provisions, which he happily shares with wayward travelers. But I fear his mother, who is an evil, ill-tempered witch. Once, long ago, I used to be a man. One day when I was out hunting, I lost my way in these mountains and wandered for days. I stumbled at last upon the Mountain Dweller's house. He welcomed me into his home and treated me like an important visitor. We feasted and talked together for days. Before long, however, his mother began to get jealous. One night, as I slept, she changed me into a mouse and tried to throw me into the fire. I ran away and have had to live ever since as the woodland creature you see before you," he finished sadly.

The girls listened carefully to the mouse's story. At the mention of feasting, their mouths watered again, for the berries had only taken the edge off their hunger. They decided to continue on through the woods to find the Mountain Dweller's house, in spite of the danger of his evil mother.

The mouse reluctantly showed the girls the right path to follow and sent them on their way with a warning.

"Do not let down your guard around the old woman," he cautioned. "If one of you sleeps, the other must stay awake to protect you both." Then the little creature scurried off into the woods.

The young women walked along the path the mouse had shown them. Before long they heard the sound of someone chopping wood.

"I wonder if that is the man Mother was talking about," said the older girl to her sister.

They followed the sound until they came to a clearing. There, standing before them, was a powerfully built man with his face painted red.

"What are you girls doing so far from home?" asked the man.

"Our mother forced us to leave," answered the girls. "She scratched us because we ate some tallow. Our mother told us, 'Because you are so fond of eating fat, you'd better go live with the Mountain Dweller.' "

The man answered, "I am the Mountain Dweller. You are welcome in my house."

Entering the man's house, they found the place very spacious and grand. He showed them another house he owned nearby, which was entirely filled with food. Seeing that they were hungry, he offered the girls something to eat and invited them to spend the night.

His mother, who also lived in the house, prepared a comfortable place for the two to sleep. The girls, mindful of the mouse's warning, took turns standing guard over each other, but the night passed without incident.

The next day both girls became his wives. For a while they all lived in contentment and plenty, the girls beginning to feel secure, for the big man slept between the two of them at night. Their mother-in-law gave them no trouble.

After a time, the food supply began to run low—the young women had tremendous appetites. The Mountain Dweller had to go off and hunt more game to provide for them all.

Before he left he warned his wives, "My mother does not let the person who stays with me live long." He gave each a sharp stick and told them to keep the weapons with them always while he was away.

One night as the girls were preparing for bed, their mother-in-law put a side of mountain sheep on the fire to cook. When it was all aflame, she tried to push it onto the girls as they pretended to sleep beside the fire. This was the way she usually killed her son's wives. But the girls were alert and watchful. With their sharp sticks, they pushed the flaming carcass right back at the old woman and killed her.

Later the Mountain Dweller came home from the hunt, loaded down with provisions. Seeing his mother's body lying on the ground, he knew what had happened. Happy though he was to find his young brides safe, he was saddened at the death of his mother.

"I need to be alone for a time," he said sadly. "Would you like to make a visit to your own parents?" he suggested. The young women had now been gone from their village for over a year, and they did miss their families. They agreed to return to their village for a visit. The Mountain Dweller hunted for a long time for an offering of meat to his father-in-law.

Then he said to his younger wife, "Make a small basket out of spruce root, just big enough to put the tip of your finger into." When the basket was finished, he shook it, and it became very large, big enough to hold all kinds of meat and sacks of tallow. Thus loading it, he shook it again, and it became small enough for the girls to carry easily.

When the girls emerged from the woods near their father's house, the first person to spot them was their younger brother. He ran into the house crying, "Mother! My sisters are outside!"

But his mother spoke to him angrily, saying, "Why do you say that? Your sisters have been dead a year, yet you say that you see them!" But the boy cried and insisted he had seen the two young women outside. His mother demanded proof. In those days, only high-caste people could wear the skin of a marten. The mother said to her son, "Go and bring me a piece of your sisters' robes."

The boy did as he was told, bringing his mother pieces of the girls' robes. When his mother and father saw the proof, they ran out of the house to greet the two girls.

"My daughters!" cried the mother, and she wept with happiness.

The next day the elder girl said to her mother, "Mother, there is a basket a little way back in the woods. We need some help bringing it to the house." All the people of the village went out to carry the basket, but it was so loaded down they could not lift it. Then the girls went out and, making the basket small again, carried it easily to their parents' house. As soon as they brought it inside, it once more became big, filled with all kinds of meats as before.

A great feast was prepared at the house of the couple and their two daughters. Everyone in the village was invited and ate their fill. They all went away very satisfied.

After a while the girls began to miss their husband, so they returned to their mountain home. As a present to their village, they left the magical basket, which stayed full of game from that time on.

Even today, if you are lost on the mountain, you have only to follow the sound of the Mountain Dweller's stone axe to get to his house. He and his wives will be happy to provide you with a hot meal and a comfortable place to sleep, if you are lucky enough to find them.

The Orphan

The winter had been hard on the Tlingit people. Sickness and famine claimed many of the clan for the spirit world. A little girl named Sahan lost her mother and father and all her brothers and sisters.

Sahan was kind and industrious, and she caught the eye of the great chief. He adopted her into his family as a companion for his only

Story collected from the mother of Katishan, chief of the Kasqague'di. Recorded in Wrangell, Alaska. She is not identified by name in source notes. Story adapted for this collection.

daughter. Each day Sahan would go to the creek to carry water back for her adoptive mother. The chief's daughter accompanied her on these trips, for she liked nothing better than to watch the changing reflections in the stream and drink deeply of the cool waters. Often the chief's daughter waded into the water and scooped handfuls of the clear liquid to her face and mouth, disturbing the peace and beauty of the reflections. "You must not drink like that," Sahan would say. "You are waking the water spirits during their time of rest. It is unlucky."

"Don't be silly. What harm can it do?" replied her companion.

And for a while it did seem like a silly superstition.

The time came for the chief's daughter to marry. Her husband was from a rich, powerful family. However, not long after the wedding, the husband's fortunes began to fail. He and his family soon became destitute. People whispered to him that it was his wife's curse that caused it. He had no choice but to abandon her.

Poor though he was, he was able to pay the meager bride price for the orphan, and in time he married Sahan, the adoptive daughter of the chief. Sahan was quiet and paid a good deal of attention to her husband, but she was also very bright and industrious. She knew how to take care of things. Before long she had made him rich again. The people of the village were pleased with her, for her husband shared his wealth with everyone.

Everything Sahan had was the best. Even her dishes and spoons were set with abalone and dentalia shells.

In the village lived Sahan's four adoptive brothers. Two were rich and two were very, very poor and unlucky. Whenever the two rich brothers came, Sahan got out her best dishes and treated them extremely well. After all, they were like her, bright, and they knew how to take care of things.

When she invited her poor brothers, her husband would say, "Get out your good dishes and let your brothers eat from them."

Sahan always answered, "I won't have my brothers use my good dishes. They might leave the mark of poverty on them."

For years Sahan continued to live her life of luxury, until late one spring, her husband died. As was the custom, her husband's relatives took away all Sahan's property, including the beautiful dishes and spoons, leaving her as destitute as she had been before. People believed that luck went against Sahan because she had treated her poor brothers so meanly.

That is why, nowadays, when a rich person has a poor brother he always treats him well.

I Am Strength

Once, all the men began to disappear from a certain village. One by one they went into the woods to gather firewood, and they never came back.

The people in the village thought there must be some monster in the woods that was killing their men. The remaining men banded together and went into the forest, planning to kill the monster.

Story collected from Kasānk, an elder Kake man. Recorded in Wrangell, Alaska. Story adapted for this collection.

Anxiously, the women and children of the village awaited the return of their loved ones. Day after day they waited, but to no avail. Their cooking fires went out for lack of firewood, and the youngest children cried from the cold. Finally, groups of women and children ventured fearfully into the woods to gather fuel, but none of these people returned either.

At last the only people left in the village were a woman and her daughter, who refused to go outside the safety of the village. The younger woman walked back and forth in front of the empty houses of her former friends, crying until her heart would break.

One day she cried so hard that the mucus flowed freely from her nose, running down her face. She wiped this off with her hand and flung it in a corner. After a while she noticed, from the corner of her eye, that the mucus moved. Curious, she peered closer and saw that it was like a bubble, with a little man inside. The young woman tried to break the bubble with her teeth, but in doing so, she accidently swallowed the little man. Before long she discovered that she was pregnant.

In due time the woman gave birth to a baby boy. This mucus child grew very fast. When he was old enough to shoot, his mother made him a little bow and arrows with which to practice. Soon he was an expert marksman.

As he grew, the boy was filled with curiosity. He asked his mother why the houses in the village were all empty, except for their own. His mother answered him: "We had many friends in this village. Now they are all gone. They went into the woods and never returned. That is why we no longer go into the forest."

The mucus child continued to grow. He was now old enough to make his own bow and arrows. His mother fashioned a quiver from deerskin for him to hold the arrows. With his new weapons he dared to venture a short way into the woods. The mucus child didn't see anything to frighten him, so he decided to go even deeper into the forest.

After traveling for some time, he reached a creek of black water which ran out from under a glacier. Sitting beside the creek was an old man, who said to the boy, "Grandson, take off all your clothes and get into the creek until the water is up to your neck. Sit there without moving, no matter how cold the water is."

The boy did as he was told. After a long time, the old man noticed small ripples moving around the boy. He thought to himself, "The water is shaking because the boy is cold."

Then the old man told the boy to come out of the water. After he had done so, the man said, "Go and try to pull up that tree over there." This tree was fairly short, and the boy pulled it up by the roots with no difficulty.

Then the old man said, "Do you see that rock over there? I want you to see if you can smash it." Again the boy did as he was told. Finally the old man told the boy to put on his clothes and return to that spot the next day.

Early the next morning the boy again met the man, who told him to get into the creek. When the old man saw the boy begin to shiver, he brought him out of the cold water. He pointed to a larger tree.

"Pull that up by the roots."

The boy pulled it up easily, although it was twice as big as the previous tree. Then the man took him to a larger rock that was shiny and hard and told him to strike it. The boy did so, shattering the rock into several pieces.

During the next four days the boy followed the old man's directions. Each day he pulled up a larger tree than the day before and crumbled larger and heavier rocks. On the fourth day the old man pulled off his own leggings, his shirt, and his moccasins, which were beautifully worked with porcupine quills, and put them on the boy.

Then he told the boy, "I am Strength. I have come to help you. Your people have been captured by the Wolf People, who live in a village at the top of the valley. Climb up the valley, keeping the glacier on your right. When you reach the top you will hear someone calling your name. It will be the Wolf People. As soon as they come within your reach, hit them with your club. The club will kill anything that it touches. Run up the hill. If you run down, they will catch you. If you get tired, think of me and you will become stronger."

The boy began climbing steadily. After a while his legs began to get weary. Resisting the urge to stop and lie down, he instead squeezed his eyes tightly shut and thought of the old man. Instantly, he felt new strength coursing through his tired legs and he pressed on, renewed.

The boy continued up the hill as he had been directed until he heard someone call. Ahead of him he saw a very large town with people running toward him. He began clubbing them as soon as they came within his reach. Although they fell heavily, he could not even feel the club strike. When the people were all destroyed, he returned to his benefactor.

When Strength heard what had happened, he said, "Go back, for there is another village on the other side of the hill. Go there and call to them, 'Give me my uncle's life, give me my village people's lives. If you don't give them to me, I will strike your village.' If they refuse, strike them with your club. If they allow you your demand, they will hand you a box."

When the boy came to the first house in the village, he asked for the lives of his townspeople, but they said, "We don't know where they are. Try the next house." He went to that house, and they also said, "We don't know where they are. Try the next house."

In each of the houses they answered him in the same manner, until he reached the last house, which belonged to the Wolf Chief. Upon the boy's request, the Wolf Chief said, "Don't strike our village. I give you the lives of your people."

The chief handed him a box and said, "Take this box back to your village and leave it in each house for four days. At the end of four days go into the house and see what has happened."

The boy followed the chief's directions and waited four days to see what would happen. Early on the morning of the fifth day, he heard noises coming from the house, so he jumped up and entered the place. There were his uncle and other relatives, walking about and looking very happy. He then left the box in all the other houses in the village until he had restored all the absent ones to life.

When all of the villagers had returned, a great celebration was held, and the brave boy who had led his people back to the land of the living sat in the place of honor.

The Girl Who Married a Bear

The basket of smoked salmon was heavy and the young girl weary as she walked gingerly along a wooded path. As she rounded the corner she barely missed some grizzly bear excrement, jumping to keep from soiling her feet. The basket slipped from her arms, spilling fish in a wide circle around her. In her frustration she spoke unkindly of bears although she knew that such words were forbidden among her people.

About a week later, in the quiet of a summer morning, she meandered by her favorite stream as she collected berries. Out of the corner of her eye she saw a movement, and at first she fearfully turned to flee. Then, across the stream, there appeared a magnificent young man. He was tall and broad shouldered and moved with the grace of a forest creature. "I have come to take you for my wife," he said. And with him she went.

The young man did not live in a traditional Tlingit plank house; rather, he lived in a dark, cool, comfortable cave. Although the girl thought this very odd, she made no mention of it. Such a place would be fine for the summer.

They passed the summer happily except for one disagreement. Her husband said that she must not turn in her sleep to look upon him until the sun was fully over the horizon.

Versions of this story appear in several sources including De Laguna (1972) and McClellan (1970). Story adapted for this collection.

Although the young woman complied with his wishes for the first two months, her curiosity finally got the best of her. One morning while pretending to sleep she rolled over and watched her husband through veiled eyes. To her horror she saw an enormous grizzly bear arise from beside her. He walked to the dark recesses of the den and took off his skin, resuming his human form. He was, in truth, the bear whom she had insulted. He had taken her away as a punishment for her unkind words.

When the bitter cold of winter came, the young woman retired to the cave with her bear-husband for their winter's sleep. During the winter she gave birth to two children. They too passed the cold of winter in gentle slumber.

At last the days grew longer and the snows began to melt. The woman, her bear-husband, and their two children left the cave to enjoy the return of life to the earth. Spring brought memories of the plank house and her human family.

As the woman watched her children she thought, "If only my Mother could hold my children. Grandfather would let them suck fat from his fingers as he did for me when I was small. My brothers would tell them stories of the clan. If we could go back, even for a few days ...," she sighed. She turned her head away from the children so they could not see her tears.

Although it was dangerous for her husband, she plotted. "My brothers hunt in these woods," she thought. "I'll leave my scent. Perhaps the dogs will bring them to us." Although she plotted well, the woman was unaware of one thing—her bear-husband's shamanistic powers. One night, in a dream, the bear saw his wife's betrayal.

One early dawn, hunting dogs could be heard baying in the distance, moving closer to their cave. Although the great bear had the power to kill the young men, he chose not to. Instead the bear prepared for his own death. Man cannot take the life of an animal without showing proper respect, so he carefully instructed his wife, "You must tell your brothers that my body must be treated in the ancient ways of my ancestors and they must sing these songs. The songs will call those who will carry me to the spirit world."

The bear stood straight as the dogs and the hunters attacked. He died with four arrows piercing his heart. The brothers prepared to resume their journey home when they came across a strange bundle of arrows outside a nearby cave. Exploring more carefully, they discovered their lost sister.

She instructed them in how they must treat her bear-husband and then said, "Please tell my mother that she must bring clothes for the children and me, for we have no human garments, only bear skins."

Her mother was overjoyed to learn that her daughter was alive and brought the requested items immediately. Although the girl longed to be with her family, she and the children had to return gradually. After living as bears they had difficulty tolerating the smell of human beings.

The following spring the young woman's youngest brother begged his sister and her children to put on their bear robes and pretend to be bears. "Please," he said. "I want to play hunter and kill a bear with my toy arrows."

"That game is not to my liking. I fear that it will come to no good," she replied. But so sweetly did the little boy beg that finally she relented. "The game seems tame enough," she decided. "What harm can come from toy arrows?"

She and the children put on their robes and frolicked on the hillside like young bear cubs. The boy in his excitement forgot the rules of the game and let a real arrow fly at one of the children. He sent one arrow after another at the terrified child. The woman turned to face her little brother. In her rage she turned into a grizzly and charged the boy. With one swipe of her giant paw, she struck him down and he rose no more.

Late that afternoon people in a nearby village saw a grizzly and her two cubs scampering up a distant hill. Never again could the bears take human form.

The lessons the young woman taught her brothers about the care of the corpse of a slain bear were passed on from one generation to the next. If the corpse is treated with proper respect, the bear will not be angry, and bear and man can live in harmony.

As for the young woman and her children, perhaps they too have passed to the world beyond, where a magnificent man, tall with broad shoulders, waits for them on the far side of the river.

Kushtaka and Witches

One thing that comes
out in myths is that
at the bottom of the
abyss comes the voice
of salvation . . . as
the darkest moment
comes to light.

—Joseph Campbell,
The Power of Myth

Kushtaka's Captive

The fishermen paddled out to sea. Hunger forced them to ignore the darkening sky and the impending rain. The winds came, then the cold, knifelike rain. The waves pitched and rolled, tossing the canoe as a child might throw a pine cone. A wave hit the front of the canoe, dumping the terrified fishermen into her dark valley. All but one of the men disappeared beneath the turbulent surface. The last man clung to a broken piece of the canoe to stay afloat.

Out of the storm a canoe came to the man. He had no time to consider whether the occupants of the canoe were friend or foe. To stay in the sea was certain death, so he allowed himself to be hoisted aboard. At first glance, the rescuers looked like ordinary men, but in reality, they were Kushtaka, sent from the land of the Not-Living-and-Not-Dead.

As the seas began to calm, the travelers pressed the canoe southward until they passed around the Queen Charlotte Islands. The Kushtaka kept a broad piece of kelp across the man to make their passage secret from him until they arrived at a place they called Rainy-village (*Sĭ-wu-á¹-ni*).

The man got out of the canoe and walked toward the Kushtaka village. He came upon a woman dressed in a groundhog robe. There was something familiar in the way she moved. At last he remembered; she was his aunt who had drowned years before.

Story collected from the mother of Katishan, chief of the Kasqague'di. Recorded in Wrangell, Alaska. She is not identified by name in source notes. Story adapted for this collection.

Glad as she was to see a relative from the other world, she did not wish her fate upon her young nephew.

She spoke in a whisper, "I cannot leave these people, for I am married to two of the Kushtaka. My human spirit lives no more. You must come to me this evening. I will see to it that my husbands help you before it is too late. You have not lived long among us, so your human spirit is still with you, although even now I see it fading. You must go quickly before you become fully Kushtaka."

The next day her husbands started back to the man's village with him. The passage across to Cape Ommaney was very difficult, for both the tide and the strong ocean currents pulled against them. They barely made it to shore before the raven called. His uncles knew that they had nearly lost their lives. Supernatural beings like the Kushtaka must be on land before the raven calls or they will be carried to the land of the dead. As soon as they came to shore, they tipped the canoe over on him, creating a prison.

The Kushtaka did not wish for him to be captured by others of their kind, so they left him near the village of Sitka. What would become of this creature who was now neither fully human nor completely Kushtaka?

The man slept by day in the nearby forests, but at night he howled, rattled smooth stones, and shrieked with chilling laughter until all the villagers were awake, trembling in their beds. Night after night he haunted the village until the villagers could stand it no more. They called a council and devised a plan to capture the man.

Snares were set up around the village, but to no avail. He broke through them as if they were nothing but the most fragile of spider webs.

An old one said, "I remember my father's father saying that the greatest enemy of the Kushtaka is the bone from a dog."

The women of the village worked all day to weave the bones of dogs into a rope to catch the Kushtaka.

Just after midnight the Kushtaka rose from his slumber to haunt the village. As he approached the first house, his body was caught in the ropes. The bones fell down upon him. He screamed with pain as the bones burned through his flesh. While he struggled to free himself, the villagers rushed out and captured him.

The old one said, "He is not as far gone as most of the victims of the Kushtaka. Give him time."

And time they gave him. The people took pity on him when they heard of his capture and the loss of his companions. After a time he became almost normal. The villagers no longer needed to surround him with dog bones.

One thing about the man did not return to normal, however. He would always eat his meat and his fish raw.

He enjoyed unfailing success as a halibut fisherman, which caused the villagers to whisper about him. They speculated that he probably learned his skill from the Kushtaka, who sometimes assumed the form of land otters.

One day, the other fishermen wished to honor the man by giving him the choicest piece of cooked halibut. At first he would not take it, but the Tlingit consider it impolite to refuse food, so he consented at last. He bit into the juicy halibut.

The people watched in horror as the food seemed to stick in his throat, choking him. In the same amount of time it took the Kushtaka to pull him from the sea, his life breath left him and he passed to the land of the dead.

As for the people, they keep their dog-bone talisman close and hope that the raven calls before another strange canoe visits their shore.

The Faithless Wife

A man of the Anga'kitān at Killisnoo kept a death watch over his beloved wife. As she lay dying, she pleaded with her husband, "Please promise me, when I die you won't bury me. The thought of the earth, dank and dark, filled with worms and maggots, is more than I can bear. I beg you, put my coffin high in the cedar until it is time for my body to be burned." As her eyes closed for the last time, the husband gave her his promise.

The poor man sobbed throughout the night. As dawn jarred him from his grief, he called for the women to prepare her body for the coffin. Then, as he had promised, he placed the coffin high in a cedar tree on a distant knoll to await cremation some weeks later.

The husband wept for a long time. At last he knew he must tend to the living. He and his wife had a small daughter who was in the care of relatives. As the sun faded, he returned to the village to take the child home.

When the village was quiet the chief's son appeared at the woman's lofty tomb and called in a whisper, "Wake up my beloved, the charade is complete."

At first there was no response. He shivered and pushed the darkest thoughts from his mind. "Perhaps the sleeping herb that produced her deathlike trance was too strong. If it has killed her, then I have no reason to live."

Story collected from the mother of Katishan, chief of the Kasqague'di. Recorded in Wrangell, Alaska. She is not identified by name in source notes. Story adapted for this collection.

The coffin moved. A hand clumsily pushed away the coffin lid. She was very much alive. He helped her down from her place of death. Both laughed quietly at how well their plan had worked. Now they were free to love each other as they had planned.

The chief's son carried her to his own house, where he kept her hidden from view. The chief could not deny his favorite son anything, so he swore the slaves to secrecy. The chief had his slaves get breakfast for the young couple long before the others in the village were up.

One morning, very early, the deceived man said to his daughter, "I have let the fire go out in the night; run out and get some fire from our neighbors." As the chief's house was the only one where she could see smoke, the little girl ran in. She stared in disbelief at what she saw. There sitting very close to the chief's son was her mother. Her mother hid her face but it was too late. The little girl ran out without speaking.

She raced home and as she gulped for air she stammered, "Father, my mother is at the chief's house. She sits with the chief's son."

He held her and said pityingly, "Poor child, your mother is dead. The woman you have seen lives only in your imagination."

The child would not be consoled. She said emphatically, "She is alive. She is not a ghost or a spirit. She is real, not from my imagination. Father, go see for yourself."

The little girl continued arguing until her father gave in, saying, "All right, we will go to the place where we put her and you will see for yourself."

The man called his brother to help him bring the box down from its high place. The box seemed light. "But bones are light," he said to himself. Opening the box, he saw, not a pile of bones, but an empty coffin.

"I have to be sure of this," he thought. About midnight a fire still burned in the chief's house. He climbed to the top of the house and peered down the smokehole. What he saw made his body shake and his hands tremble. There was his beloved wife gazing happily at her new love as she snuggled beneath his martenskin robe.

"What can I do? I must become a wizard and use my witching powers to destroy them both. Then I shall see how death rests upon her," he muttered to no one.

He walked to the sacred graveyard of the shamans to sit among the bodies and bones of the dead. So overwrought was he that he violated a sacred taboo. He desecrated the remains of the dead. He rubbed the bones of the shaman over his body until at last he found two shoulder blades. He fanned and rubbed himself until he fainted. When he awoke he found that he could use them like wings. He swooped through the night like an owl looking for prey.

The wings took him into the woods where he cut two very hard limbs. After sharpening the limbs he soaked them in bear grease and burned the points to make them even harder. With his weapons in hand he flew to the roof of the chief's house and passed through the smokehole. He bewitched everyone in the house so that they slept soundly. Then he moved quietly to the room where his wife and the chief's son slept, and, with two mighty thrusts, he pierced their hearts.

Early the next morning the slaves got up as usual to wait upon the young people. As morning gave way to noonday the young people had not yet risen. Finally the slaves entered the room and saw them lying in each other's arms. Blood covered the martenskin robe. They would rise no more.

The news spread throughout the village. The same morning, the woman's former husband took his gambling sticks and went out to join his companions. He pretended that he knew nothing of what happened, although his friends thought his behavior strange. In the midst of gambling he would call out, "Sharp sticks, oh, yes, very sharp sticks. Yes, yes, sharp sticks."

The last time his friends saw him he was playing with the bones in the graveyard. He had a happy although vacant look about him. People thought they heard him saying, "Oh, happy wings and sharp sticks, happy sticks. Happy sticks and sharp wings. Fly away away. Fly away."

Epilogue

I was silent.
My pipe had gone out.

—J. Frederic Thorne
(*In the Time That Was;*
Being Legends of the Alaska Klingits)

And at last, the story is finished.

Reference List

Abraham, Olaf. 1973. *Yakulat History, Haa Kusteeyee Aya'.* Translated by Elaine Ramos. Sitka, Alaska: Sheldon Jackson College.

Beck, Mary Giraudo. 1991. *Shamans and Kushtakas.* Anchorage, Alaska: Alaska Northwest Books.

Billman, Esther. 1970. "A Study of the Elements of the Supernatural among the Tlingit of Sitka and Yakuta." Master's thesis, Sheldon Jackson College, Sitka, Alaska.

Corey, Peter. 1985. *Wonderful Heroes, Fearsome Creatures: Art of the Northwest Coast.* Clinton, N.Y.: Fred L. Emerson Galleries of Hamilton College.

Campbell, Joseph. 1968. *The Hero with a Thousand Faces.* 2d ed. Princeton, N.J.: Princeton University Press.

Campbell, Joseph, with Bill Moyers. 1988. *The Power of Myth.* New York: Doubleday.

Dauenhauer, Nora Marks, and Richard Dauenhauer, eds. 1987. *Haa Shuká, Our Ancestors: Tlingit Oral Narratives.* Seattle: University of Washington Press.

_____. 1990. *Haa Tuwunaagu Yis, For Healing Our Spirit: Tlingit Oratory.* Seattle: University of Washington Press; Juneau, Alaska: Sealaska Heritage Foundation.

De Laguna, Frederica. 1956. "Childhood among the Yakutat Tlingits." In *Context and Meaning in Cultural Anthropology*, edited by Melford Spiro. New York: Free Press.

————. 1972. *Under Mount Saint Elias: The History and Culture of Yakutat Tlingit.* Smithsonian Contributions to Anthropology. Vol. 7 (in 3 parts). Washington, D.C.: Smithsonian Institution Press.

Garfield, Viola. 1967. *Meet the Totem.* Revised ed. Sitka, Alaska: Sitka Printing Company.

George, Judy. 1992. Personal communication. Juneau, Alaska.

Gunther, Erna. 1972. *The Indian Life of the Northwest Coast of North America.* Chicago: University of Chicago Press.

Hall, Betty. 1984. *Totemic Design and Forms.* Ketchikan, Alaska: Betty's Rainbow Press.

Holden, Glenn. 1973. *Talking Totem Poles.* New York: Dodd, Mead.

Holm, Bill. 1989. *Northwest Coast Indian Art.* Seattle: University of Washington Press.

Holmberg, Heinrich Johan. 1985. *Holmberg's Ethnographic Sketches.* Edited by Marvin W. Falk. Translated by Fritz Jaensch. Fairbanks: University of Alaska Press. Originally published in Russian, 1855-1863.

Hope, Andrew, III. 1982. *Raven's Bones.* Sitka, Alaska: Sitka Community Association.

Hunt, Norma Bancroft, and Werner Forman. 1979. *People of the Totem: The Indians of the Pacific Northwest.* New York: G. P. Putnam's.

James, George Wharton. 1972. *Indian Basketry.* New York: Dover Publications.

Kamenskii, Anatolei. 1985. *Tlingit Indians of Alaska.* Translated by Sergei Kan. Fairbanks: University of Alaska Press. Original Russian edition, 1840.

Kan, Sergei. 1989. *Symbolic Immortality: Tlingit Potlatch of the Nineteenth Century.* Washington, D.C.: Smithsonian Institution Press.

Keithahn, Edward. 1962. *Monuments in Cedar.* New York: Bonanza Books.

Knapp, Marilyn. 1980. *Carved History: The Totem Poles and House Posts of Sitka National Park.* Anchorage, Alaska: Alaska National History Association.

Krause, Aurel. 1956. *The Tlingit Indians.* Translated by Erna Gunther. Seattle: University of Washington Press.

McClellan, Catharine. 1970. *The Girl Who Married a Bear, a Masterpiece of Indian Oral Tradition.* Ottawa, Canada: National Museum of Ottawa.

Miller, Polly, and Leon Miller. 1967. *Lost Heritage of Alaska.* Cleveland, Ohio: World Publishing.

Oberg, Kalvero. 1973. *The Social Economy of the Tlingit Indians.* Seattle: University of Washington Press.

Olson, R. L. 1967. *Social Structure and Social Life of Tlingits in Alaska.* Anthropological Records. Vol. 26. Berkeley: University of California Press.

————. 1956. "Channeling of Character in Tlingit Society." In *Personal Character and Cultural Milieu.* Edited by Douglas G. Haring. New York: Syracuse University Press.

Paul, Frances. 1944. *Spruce Root Basketry of the Alaska Tlingit.* Lawrence, Kans.: U.S. Department of the Interior.

Peck, Cyrus E. 1975. *The Tides People: Tlingit Indians of Southeastern Alaska.* Juneau, Alaska: City and Borough of Juneau School District.

Salisbury, O. M. 1962. *The Customs and Legends of the Thlinget Indians of Alaska.* New York: Bonanza Books.

Samuel, Cheryl. 1987. *The Raven's Tail.* Vancouver, Canada: University of British Columbia Press.

Stewart, Hilary. 1979. *Looking at Indian Art of the Northwest Coast.* Seattle: University of Washington Press.

Swanton, John. 1970. *Social Conditions, Beliefs, and Linguistic Relationship of the Tlingit Indians.* New York: Johnson Reprint. Original publication, 1908.

———. 1909. *Tlingit Myths and Texts.* Bureau of American Ethnology Bulletin 39. Washington, D.C.: Smithsonian Institution.

———. 1927. "A Return from the Spirit Land: The Legend of the Tlingit Orpheus." *Alaska Magazine* 1 (February): 57.

Thorne, J. Frederic. 1909. *In the Time That Was; Being Legends of the Alaska Klingits.* Seattle, Wash.: Gateway Printing.

Veniaminov, Ivan. 1984. *Notes on the Islands of the Unalashka District.* Translated by Lydia T. Black and R. H. Geoghegan. Edited with an introduction by Richard A. Pierce. Ontario, Canada: Kingston Limestone. Original publication in Russia, 1840.

Index

About the Authors

Mary Helen Hamilton Pelton (left) and Jacqueline Hamilton DiGennaro (right) are sisters who grew up in Owatonna, Minnesota.

Mary Helen Pelton is the Assistant Dean of Continuing Education at the University of North Dakota and is a well-known professional storyteller. She received her B.A. from Emory University in Atlanta, Georgia, and her M.A. and Ed.D. from the University of Denver, Colorado.

Through the University of North Dakota, she teaches the art of storytelling to teachers, children, and community members and has coauthored a book published by Libraries Unlimited titled *Every Child a Storyteller: A Handbook of Ideas* (1991). As both a lover and a student of "story," Pelton was drawn to the rich cultural history and the compelling tales of the Tlingit.

Jacqueline DiGennaro is an elementary school teacher and writer. She teaches in a multicultural classroom in Sitka, Alaska, and has been living and working in southeastern Alaska since 1979. A deep appreciation for Tlingit culture and an interest in recording some of their colorful stories motivated her to coauthor this book.

DiGennaro is presently working on a historically based novel for children, set in Sitka. *Images of a People* is her first major publication.

About the Illustrator

Jennifer Brady-Morales is a Tlingit/Tsimshian artist who does traditional northwest coast native style art. Raised in Sitka, Alaska, Jennifer's Tlingit name is *Ts'anak* and her borrowed name is Jennifer Brady. She was named for a high-caste Tlingit woman who died during the time of the Russian-Kiksadi battle in 1804. Ts'anak is descended from Anahootz Jackson, last chief, or "Big Man," of the Kaagwaantaan. She is also the great-niece of Rudolph Walton, a Kiksadi carver, who was also a chief.

Ts'anak has been carving, painting, and designing since 1981. She works in silver, wood, and ivory, and she also designs, paints, and creates rawhide drums for dancing and display. Her flatwork includes posters, cards, logos, and silkscreen prints. She credits northwest coast artists Nathan Jackson, Steve Brown, Darryl Norman, Dorthea Romero Norman, and Ketchikan artist Norman Jackson as instructors. She has also been influenced by artists Will Burkhart, Wayne Price, Reggie Peterson, and Robert Davidson. Ts'anak was first exposed to art by her father, Gunaanasti, who is a carver.

Besides art owned by private collectors, pieces of her work are on display at the N. B. A. Museum in Anchorage, Alaska; the Egan Library, University of Alaska, Juneau; and the Smithsonian Institution in Washington, D.C.